THE POET
AUDEN

THE POET
AUDEN

A Personal Memoir

A.L. ROWSE

WEIDENFELD & NICOLSON
New York

Published by Weidenfeld & Nicolson, New York
A Division of Wheatland Corporation
10 East 53rd Street
New York, New York 10022

First published in Great Britain in 1987 by Methuen Ltd.

Library of Congress Cataloging-in-Publication Data

Rowse, A.L. (Alfred Leslie), 1903–
    The poet Auden: a personal memoir / A.L. Rowse.—1st ed.
    p.   cm.
    ISBN 1-555-84198-8
    1. Auden, W.H. (Wystan Hugh), 1907–1973—Biography.
2 Poets, English—20th century—Biography. 3. Rowse, A.L.
(Alfred Leslie), 1903–   —Friends and associates. I. Title.
PR6001.U4Z795 1988
811'.52—dc19
[B]   87-33975
                                                                       CIP

Manufactured in the United States of America

First American Edition, 1988

10 9 8 7 6 5 4 3 2 1

To
Charles Monteith
Wystan's Friend and Mine

Contents

1

The Man

I knew Auden from the time he was an undergraduate, 1925–8, at my own old college, Christ Church, Oxford, where I had been the English Literature Scholar in the previous undergraduate generation, 1922–5. So I was three years his senior. That makes all the difference at the university: seniority draws a line, and that prevailed all through our lives right up to his return to Oxford at the end.

As he himself says, the House[1] was snooty about English Literature as a subject for Schools, regarding it as a soft option taken mainly by women (as it was then). The College had no teaching job in the subject, though I could have been appointed later, had I wished. Meanwhile the dons put me through the History School, which I found uphill work – I had not expected that, and was more geared to literature, especially poetry, which I continued to write, in spite of the enormous amount of historical reading to get through. I should have been more grateful than I was, for it was only that which enabled me to win a Prize Fellowship at All Souls at the end of it.

Auden also switched, of his own volition, from the Natural Science he originally intended to English Literature. Since Christ Church didn't teach it, hardly recognised it as an academic subject, he was farmed out to be taught by Nevill Coghill of Exeter College. Nevill was a man of creative gifts, a remarkable producer of plays, and eventually came to write on his own – modernising Chaucer's *Canterbury Tales*, for example, and making a play out of them. This

---

[1] Christ Church is referred to as the House, from its Latin name *Aedes Christi*.

was successful in London. I was in the plane with him when he went over to New York, where the play did not take. Nevill once said to me that, though he had written thousands of lines of verse, he had never written a line of poetry. They are indeed different things. Wystan, like his undergraduate contemporary and friend Betjeman, could do both.

He became a close, and even intimate, friend of Nevill, with whom I was friendly up to his death – still more so with John Betjeman, to whose personality and poetry I was really always more sympathetic. It was to Nevill that the young tyro, his pupil, said that he meant to become 'a great poet'. Did he become one? That is what we must find out in the course of this study.

From the very first I had no doubt of his genius. He would come to All Souls, his pockets stuffed with manuscripts of his poems to read to me and – though not the idiom I was used to, not even Eliot – I could recognise a new and individual voice. My diary records lunching with him in his rooms in Peckwater V.5 in October 1926 and October 1927; and his lunching with me in February 1928 to meet a couple of my friends – doing my bit to put him across. Then I have him to dine, or again tea, at All Souls that July.

Oddly enough, I have no memory of these occasions. It is understandable that the one occasion I have never forgotten is that written up in the biographies of him, though only I know the (perhaps absurd) story of it. It is still vivid in my memory after all those years. After a poetry reading in the hot glare of summer sun in the inner quad at All Souls, Wystan suggested that we should adjourn to his rooms in Peck and continue. Arrived there, he proceeded to 'sport the oak' (shut the outer door), pull down the blinds and close the shutters, turn on the green-shaded light on his desk – and read to me, not poems, but letters from a friend of his in Mexico, employed in the Eagle Oil Company, about his goings-on with the boys.

This was a quite unexpected development. After all, I had not been at a public school, but an innocent, small grammar school – co-educational too – and was *years* behind these contemporaries in experience of the facts of life, let alone sophistication, everything. (It took me an age to catch up with them; I've been competing with them and against the advantages they had all my life.)

Ingenuous rather than priggish, all the same no fool, I recognised the situation and was not giving myself away. The reader must recognise the immense difference that belonging to another generation makes at the university. Wystan was my junior, and I was already a don, very conscious of my status as such, perhaps all the more so because youthfully attained against such odds. Anyhow, as I sank defensively back deep into my armchair I wondered how I could get out of the situation with dignity, reflecting (ludicrously enough) to myself, 'Fellows of All Souls don't do that sort of thing.'

At that Tom came to my rescue: the great bell of Yeats's poem boomed through the quad. 'Four o'clock,' I said, 'I'm always in the Common Room at All Souls for tea at four', and got away.

Wystan was never quite on all fours with me – if, in the circumstances, the expression may be pardoned – for years after that, really until he came back to Oxford at the end of his life, and I took him under my wing again at All Souls. It had drawn an invisible line. We never discussed the matter; but the fact was that, though my sympathies were with them, I was not one of the boys. It was not a question of morals, but of taste and *tenue*, of the way to behave. After all, Wystan was himself to write:

> Private faces in public places
> Are wiser and nicer
> Than public faces in private places.

In my view private life should be kept private, not brandished in public – too vulgar and undignified. I have never had any sympathy with Wilde's vulgar Irish exhibitionism, asking for trouble and bringing down untold (and unnecessary) suffering, even death, upon hundreds, if not thousands, of people. Unforgivable.

Here is the place to confront at the outset the prime question in Wystan's life, and to treat it from a rational point of view. I state the principle from which I regard it in the terms of the philosophic theologian, Bishop Butler: 'Things are what they are, and their consequences will be what they will be: why should we seek to be deceived?'

For 'things' we might read men (and women). Moreover, the

clumsy categories of ordinary people do not apply, as in most things, to men of genius – or women, say, Vita Sackville-West and Virginia Woolf. These matters are more complex than such categories can contain, or conventional fools comprehend. My generation was much more mixed-up and troubled, rendered unhappy by them, riven by guilt – as John Betjeman was, for example.

The really remarkable thing about Wystan was that he should have accepted the fact about his own nature when he was a schoolboy – quite naturally and rationally, without any fuss. This was very precocious of him, and courageous; of course, he was precocious intellectually and had plenty of courage, though – oddly – the acceptance of what his nature was does not seem to have required much courage in his case. He was lucky.

He was dominantly, though not exclusively, homosexual, let alone devoutly – as Isherwood was (apparently by act of will rather than of nature – odder still, if so). Later on, in New York, Wystan lived happily and affectionately for a time with a woman friend. I have sometimes wondered whether he would not have been happier as a family man, with wife and children. For he needed a family: he was lonely, for all his gregariousness and friends, and came to be deeply unhappy. He did not have Philip Larkin's horror of the family, of wife and children – when Philip was entirely heterosexual. One sees how complicated things are with men of genius. Philip utterly rejected family life; Wystan early took a path that led away from it, and may have missed it.

His great need was to be loved. I think that that came from his having been spoiled as a child, the youngest, by doting parents, especially by Mother. (He took after her; she was always there as the dominant influence *behind* his life. Her death brought him back to the Church of his childhood. Even as an elderly man 'Mother wouldn't like it', frequently on his lips, settled matters for him.)

He had an almost equal need to love someone. This was the fundamental fact of his long, not ultimately satisfactory, relationship with Chester Kallman; for Chester, though fond of him and dependent on him, was not in love with him. Here was an imbalance, and a need unsatisfied at the bottom of Wystan's sad unhappiness.

I do wish he could have found a way to be happier; but so much of poetry comes out of this maladjustment, this *malaise*, this rift. Philip Larkin held that all poetry that was any good sprang from sadness. This was generalising from his own experience. Still, it is true that Eliot would not have written much but for his inner misery – and, when at length he found happiness, the poetry went.

A prime subject, or issue, of Auden's poetry is love, from the early oracular statement, 'We must love one another, or die' – which he later questioned and altered, right on to the long prose piece he wrote, in place of a love poem, discussing the nature of love and what he meant by it. I find the piece confused and confusing. The subject, too vast and complex, is not one for definition. Far better are Auden's simplest love lyrics, the best poetry he ever wrote.

He wrote verse of any and every kind, with extreme virtuosity, from the noble and inspired to the lowest music-hall catches, limericks, clerihews. With his exceptional self-awareness he knew that he was 'intuitive rather than analytic' – so why all that attempt at analysing what love is, what it is to be 'in love', etc? Nor do I think highly of sententious poetry, i.e. poetry that argues. Shakespeare's gnomic verse is but verse, for argument is fundamentally a prose function. Even here one must allow that Auden had an exceptional gift. To be able to carry on an argument in verse, as he does in *New Year Letter* for example, is very remarkable.

There goes along with this far too much rhetoric. He recognised this himself and, in continually revising early work, conscientiously tried to get rid of, or at least reduce, rhetoric where he could. All his life he was given to being oracular, laying down the law. In so far as intuition gave him a sudden insight, that serves; but it became a trick – not only that, but more, a habit. Again, in earlier days, he recognised the foible, and asked why people took his pronounce-ments so seriously. (Life in America encouraged this tendency – led to what Larkin called, unkindly and I think unfairly, the 'windbag'.)

I must return to my own experience with him. Everybody knew that there was a bossy side to him – it was what led to the eventual breach with Britten. For myself, I never once met it. Here is where seniority, the difference of generation, came in – far more operative among university people than is generally realised. Wystan's attitude to me was respectful, if not positively deferential – there *was* something of that at the end as at the beginning. He was schoolmasterish, everybody recognised; very well, I was donnish. He spent years and years as a schoolmaster in Britain and again in the United States; I spent all my life as a don. He had a message to put across; so had I – so we both laid down the law in our respective circles. Both of us ended in disillusionment – and a remarkable degree of agreement.

Here I am bound to make an unworthy confession: I always held his Third in the Schools against him. That was a natural donnish attitude, but it was more than that. As a grammar school boy I had worked hard to get about the best First of my year in the History School, which I did not find altogether congenial. I disapproved of all these bright sparks of my (literary) acquaintance who did no work, got Thirds in the Schools, like Connolly, Waugh, Wystan – or got sent down, like Peter Quennell (my opposite number as Eng. Lit. Scholar at Balliol) and John Betjeman.

I thought them wasters; and Wystan did have a feeling of guilt all the time he was neglecting to do any work for Schools. People have expressed wonder at how he could get a Third, when he was as clever as a monkey: this is how. Where I was wrong was in this: with a don's standards I tended henceforth to disconsider him intellectually.

It hardly needs saying now that he had first-rate intelligence, great vivacity of intellect – besides his genius, a gift – and quite exceptional width of reading and reflection. Of course he had a first-class mind, at work in prose as in poetry (where 'intellect' is not of prime importance, may even get in the way, as it did with him). But he was not a scholar: he did not slowly, patiently, *think things through*.

This is where he was apt to go wrong, and get things wrong: his critical judgment was rather hit-or-miss. Unlike his friend Louis MacNeice, perhaps a less original, certainly less originating mind, but a trained mind and a better critic.

This may be illustrated by a different opinion which Auden held to and insisted on, which I think – as any historian would (he was no historian) – to be not only wrong-headed (he was perverse), but obvious nonsense. In our time at Oxford the Eng. Lit. fashion was to depreciate and ignore the personal and biographical element in considering literature. The bullying figure of C.S. Lewis called this the 'Personal Heresy' – anything he disagreed with was of course 'heresy'. My friend David Cecil, also a figure in the Eng. Lit. School, did not subscribe to this nonsense – he had taken the History School and had historical common sense in the matter, but had nothing like Lewis's intellectual force and influence.

Behind this anti-personal nonsense loomed the grand guru Eliot, who regularly enforced that the personal, in considering works of literature, and therefore in criticism, was not to be taken into account. The joke was that anything more acutely personal, more autobiographical than his own work, would be hard to find: one positively needs to know the background of his own life and circumstances to interpret it.

This needs no emphasising to any historian – merely common sense. But, beneath the elimination of the biographical element, the writer's life, the Eng. Lit. fashion had a point, only it wasn't stated clearly. Of course the critical *judgment* of a work was something separate from the circumstances that went into it, the biographical and personal, the facts of a writer's or artist's life. Even so, allowing that, is the critical estimate entirely divorced from the *content* of the work? On the side of common sense it can be said that all the relevant facts help to illuminate the work, and it is a historian's business to know everything.

We see that behind this dispute is a simple intellectual confusion: that critical estimation and judgment are something separate from the information making towards it, though even so, relevant information contributes, in varying degrees, to interpretation – in my view an essential service of literary criticism.

Hence it is offensive to common sense to see the absolute prohibition which Auden places upon the biographical and personal. 'Not only would most genuine writers prefer to have no biography written, they would also prefer, were it practically feasible, that their writings were published anonymously.' Again, 'If the Muses could lobby for their interest, all biographical research into the lives of artists would probably be prohibited by law, and historians of the individual would have to confine themselves to those who act but do not make.' The qualification gives the argument away – apart from the loss we should suffer without Dr Johnson's Lives of the English Poets, or Vasari's Lives of the Renaissance Painters, or Plutarch who provided Shakespeare with so much.

This curious obscurantism, not wanting to know, or even wanting not to know – criminal to an historian, if it were not so silly – contradicts itself in the end. And this we find with Auden when he comes to consider Cavafy: 'Reading any poem of his I feel: "This reveals a person with a unique perspective on the world." ' Well, exactly: we need to know what we can find out about him to understand the poem fully.

This abnegation of knowledge has the worst consequences when we come to Shakespeare. Auden lays down that 'Shakespeare is in the singularly fortunate position of being, to all intents and purposes, anonymous.' He is then surprised to find that Freud subscribed to the rubbish that the Earl of Oxford wrote Shakespeare's plays for him. But if a man doesn't *know*, is prohibited from knowing, he can think any nonsense. Actually, he doesn't qualify to hold an opinion unless he knows, and he will probably get it wrong.

Indeed, Auden was largely wrong about the Sonnets. 'It so happens that we know almost nothing about the historical circumstances under which Shakespeare wrote these Sonnets; we don't know to whom they are addressed or exactly when they were written, and – unless entirely new evidence should turn up, which is unlikely – we never shall.'

Every one of these statements is incorrect, as we now know. We know the dating and the historical circumstances, to whom they were addressed and when they were written. Most people don't know, evidently Wystan didn't, that in fact we know more about William Shakespeare than about any other Elizabethan dramatist, except for the later life of Ben Jonson – and we know far more about Shakespeare's earlier life than of Jonson's. And all with good reason. A real Elizabethan scholar knows this – Auden was not a scholar, and it made me wickedly recall his Third in the Schools. He did not get down to the dull, laborious grind of *thinking things through* and *finding out*.

If one doesn't do that – most people are incapable of it anyway –

one is liable to fall for any nonsense, the plays written by Oxford or Bacon, or possibly Queen Elizabeth under an assumed name. A real scholar wants to *know*. Denial or rejection of knowledge, historical, biographical or personal, leads to this sort of muddle and confusion. One of my last talks with Wystan was on this subject. I suppose I was holding forth about my findings on Shakespeare. He must have known my line, but had, as usual, not gone into it. He merely said, apologetically, almost submissively, 'You know I am not for the personal approach. . . .' I didn't pursue the matter, for I didn't, and don't, take him seriously on a matter of scholarship.

It reveals too an element that was constant in his make-up – just prejudice, or preconception: he would take up a position and stick to it, without going into it. A scholar has to be more flexible, and revise his conclusions in accordance with the evidence. Wystan was prejudiced against France and French culture; he took up this position when quite young, a schoolboy, and never revised it. He opted for Germany, language, literature and (more understandably) music. He says that he did it by way of reaction against the pro-French leanings of the previous generation.

Here was a real ground of disagreement I had with all his group. I thought that French discipline, the classic standards of French literature and art, the clarity of the language, were just what Auden–Spender–Isherwood needed. Instead of that they went in for horrible German Expressionismus, the indiscipline of the Weimar Republic, the unspeakable vulgarity of Berlin. Think of it, opting for Berlin as against Paris!

Of course Wystan was Nordic, flaxen-haired with fair skin, a blond, so he had instinctive leanings that way already – which provides another reason for providing a Latin corrective. They wouldn't have it, they all went whoring (if that is the word for it) after beastly Berlin and Rügen Island, the theatre of the evil-minded Brecht, the ego-mania of Rilke and Thomas Mann, who thought himself not only Goethe but God.

The standards of French literature would have been much better for their own writing. No doubt they would have thought that typically donnish of me, and they certainly wouldn't have taken it from me. For here comes in another point, not very important, but it

was there. They were really rather anti-academic – perhaps understandably, after they had done so badly at and by the university.

Isherwood hated Cambridge – fancy anybody hating so beautiful
a place, young ass! I met him only once, at Oxford, when he spent an
afternoon with me at All Souls; he looked like a spinster governess,
immensely neat – unlike the shambling, grubby Wystan – hair parted
genteelly down the middle, prissy lips. (He later got a mouth
infection; I don't wonder.) We had nothing to say to each other; I
dare say he got me framed – 'I am a Camera' – as Don, the enemy. In
all the later years I spent in Los Angeles he never made an approach,
nor I to him – though I used to hear plenty about his goings-on on the
neighbouring campuses, private life rendered all too public.

They all wrote each other up like mad – again understandably:
needs must, for they were out in the world scrabbling for a living and
needed the publicity. I didn't, for I was safe and secure at All Souls,
sheltered in the world of academe and scholarship, aligned with
Housman not Auden. Today, they are grossly over-written, especially Isherwood – Herr Issyvoo and all that: I doubt if much of him
will remain.

The one original genius among them all – certainly not Day Lewis
– was Auden. After all the writing him up, Stephen Spender wonders
whether he really liked him. I can honestly say that I have a feeling of
affection for him, a protective elder-brotherly feeling. He aroused
affection among a great many people, he had a wide cosmopolitan
circle of friends, perhaps too many – rather undiscriminating of him.

Yet it was never enough: from early days as a writer there was this
feeling of being unloved. It was indeed difficult to 'love' him, with all
those squalid habits: the perpetual cigarette-smoking, filthy fags
never away from his lips, fingers stained with nicotine, nails bitten to
the quick; cigarette ash scattered down his front, all around
wherever he was – no wonder he weakened his heart; untidiness
everywhere, he reduced any room he was in to a shambles, picking
up coats and even carpets to pile on top of his bed; then the drink, of
every kind, the necessity for it, apart from a little drug in the morning
and another at night. No wonder Chester couldn't love him, for all
that Wystan did for him; with my donnish insistence on tidiness, let
alone an aesthete's determination to have everything proper and

handsome about me, I couldn't put up with him in the house for a single day. He wasn't house-trained. How on earth can he have got like that? No woman would have put up with it.

Yet he was good and kind and a Christian gentleman – no cad, like plenty of people in literary life, his great admirer Grigson for one. And underneath the exotic personality, the strangeness, was a fund of common sense – which makes his departures from it the more conspicuous.

The strangest thing about the personality and the work is something that John Bayley shrewdly noticed: the sense of rarely being in touch with the inner man, the impersonal feeling, the distance kept. For all Eliot's supposed obscurity – he is never so obscure as people (and he) made out – one is always in touch with the inner man. With Wystan rarely, only fully in the early lyrics and the few direct love poems.

All the rest he *willed*. He meant to be 'a great poet'. But one can't write poetry by willing it, for all his marvellous gift for words and metrics. Poetry comes from a deeper level, and is given to one: the intellect but shapes it up. In most of contemporary uncooked poetry there is not even intellect to shape it up. Plenty of intelligence and form and words, words, words in Auden; but how much of the heart?

Larkin thought that Thomas Hardy spoke the truth about poetry when he said that it was language from the heart expressed rhythmically in such a way as to move other hearts. *Und sonst nichts*. How much of Auden's voluminous, prolific work moves the heart? Or even the mind? Eliot said when *For the Time Being* came to him for publication, that he was impressed by it but was not sure that he could understand it. Neither can I – and I am not impressed by what I cannot understand. Desmond MacCarthy made a suggestion to the young Auden which he would have done well to take to heart – namely, that instead of setting himself to be mysteriously impressive he should aim at making himself clear.

I regard that as the aim of good writing, the aim of criticism to clarify and interpret, to express what is thought in simpler terms, not to make it more opaque. Auden took the opposite line. It was not merely a question of rare and obscure words, though he sought them out, writing always with a dictionary within reach. The trouble is at a deeper level: I suspect that he was not *thinking through* what he was saying. He was an incredibly fast and facile, as well as verbally gifted, writer and he wrote far too much for a poet.

Most professional poets write too much. Look at Browning! – another case of needless obscurity. Tennyson wrote too much, so did Wordsworth, Swinburne, William Morris, Shelley, even aesthetes like Keats or Bridges . I do not mean to limit poetry to the ideal of 'la poésie pure' of Valéry and Mallarmé, or, for that matter, of Rilke or Stefan George. There are different kinds of poetry, but most of what is written on a large scale is just verse. And that is true for Auden as for Browning or Byron.

So I have proposed myself a difficult task in this study, even apart from the difficulty of the subject in itself. I do not wish to duplicate work done in two excellent biographies, which give the facts and are properly sympathetic, Charles Osborne's and Humphrey Carpenter's. A third book is valuable, *W.H. Auden: A Tribute*, edited by Stephen Spender, with many contributions by friends, and a useful chronology by Edward Mendelson.

What I wish to do is, I hope, more original: to sleuth him in his work. For all Wystan's failure to catch up with it, I have managed to sleuth William Shakespeare in his,[1] and to reduce the so-called problems or, rather, the confusions that have been made of his life and work, to common sense. Wystan disesteemed the personal, wanted no biography of himself written (any more than I do), and made things as difficult as he could. To track down the poet in his work, spring him out of his lair, may not be sport, but it should be fun.

[1] cf. my *Shakespeare's Self-Portrait*.

2

The Thirties

In his last year as an undergraduate, 1928, Wystan had a tiny volume of his poems printed, by Spender on a hand press, only forty copies, for one of which I faithfully subscribed. Carpenter says that I was 'made to pay' – but I was only too glad to do so, do my duty to help a coming young poet who was a friend. It must have contained some of the poems Wystan had read to me. I cannot now tell, for I lent the little brochure to a young *protégé*, who disappeared. So did the book, a collector's piece now worth thousands.

In those days I was always lending out books. The moral I draw from this regrettable episode – the poems were anyway lost on the *protégé* – is: Never Lend a Book. Somebody was once shown into a friend's library and admired the books; to which the friend replied, 'All these books were borrowed once.'

Wystan spent 1928–9 in Germany, his first year there. I heard news of him only occasionally – for example, shovelling snow in the streets of Berlin to earn a pittance and shack up with the proletariat. I didn't need that: I was a proletarian already. And an active, practical Labour Party man – partly out of pride: I wouldn't have it said that, just because I had gone to Oxford, I had gone over to the Tories. In fact, much influenced by Marxism, I became a fanatic with a Message, though with too much working-class horse-sense ever to become a Communist.

A proselytiser, I remember wrestling for the soul of Stephen Spender as a recruit for the Labour Party. Not a bit of it: he was bent on becoming a Communist. I tried to recruit Middleton Murry: no luck, he went and joined the already sinking ILP (Independent Labour Party), a fractious group to the Left of the main Party, 'led' by the hopeless, long-haired Jimmy Maxton, on the way out. What was the matter with these middle-class intellectuals? Why had they no practical common sense, let alone political sense? Though an intellectual myself, I shared Ernest Bevin's view of them. Wystan was lined up with them, but, remarkably, as I have said, he had more common sense. He didn't really know much about Marx; he hadn't read much of Marxism, in which I was well versed and had a whole Marxist library. He was much better read in Freud, as I was not – and a fat lot of good that did him.

1929 was the year in which a Labour government took office, with the Party the largest number in the Commons, though still a minority, dependent on the divided Liberals. We were young then, with hopes of social democracy giving a lead from this country to Europe – disarmament, peace and all that. I wrote my book *Politics and the Younger Generation* putting forward the message I had it in my guts to deliver.

Eliot was very good about it, considering how little he agreed with it; accepted it for publication, went through it carefully and precisely with his sharp-pointed pencil, and came down to All Souls to go through it with me.[1]

All to no point. MacDonald's government was caught in the World Economic Crisis by the steep rise in unemployment and the run on the pound. At the General Election in 1931 both Tories and Liberals ganged up to do Labour in, who returned 55 MPs to over 500 supporters of the bogus 'National' government. That unspeakable assembly was in control of Parliament and British politics throughout the thirties, and could have done anything necessary in the interests of the country. In fact it proceeded to betray them, and stumbled from betrayal to betrayal to the precipice of 1939.

The disastrous Election of 1931 was my first experience as a political candidate, standing for my home division in Cornwall. It was a miserably enlightening experience. The electorate allowed

---

[1] I have written an essay about that experience, 'Eliot Fifty Years After', *Yale Magazine*.

itself to be panicked again, as it had been by the Red Letter scare in 1924. At that time, an ingenuous undergraduate, I had been astonished that the people could be such fools. In 1931, I had no illusions about the masses; even so I was a bit shocked by the trickery resorted to. For a week before the polls, the local daily, *The Western Morning News*, featured the juiciest passages from my book – up-to-date opinions about religion and sex – to scare away Nonconformist voters. They do not seem to have scared many, but the book itself was a casualty of that decisive year 1931, when all hopes in Britain were reversed, and its programme no longer applied.

1929 had been a false dawn. It is necessary to say as much to make clear the background to the thirties, Wystan's work throughout that appalling decade, and the ultimate upshot for him – leaving the disgraced country for America:

> On Fifty-second street
> Uncertain and afraid
> As the clever hopes expire
> Of a low dishonest decade.

Well, exactly.

In 1930 Eliot published Auden's *Paid on Both Sides: A Charade* in *The Criterion*. He had announced 'a new form of literary award to be conferred by five reviews: *The Criterion*, the *Europaeische Revue* of Berlin, the *Nouvelle Revue Française* of Paris, the *Revista de Occidente* of Madrid, and the *Nuova Antologia* of Milan'. Here was civilised Mandarin Europe, to be destroyed in 1933, though Eliot went on with his literary organ, his pulpit, putting an immense amount of hard work into it until he gave up in despair in 1939.

He had recruited me to the team two or three years before, and kept me reviewing books on history and politics, pressing me to write on Marxism, Communism, etc. In this number I was reviewing A.F. Pollard's *Wolsey* and a book on the great German industrialist, Walther Rathenau, in whose work I was much interested as being half-way to socialism. His enormous ability had organised Germany's economy so as to enable her to survive in the war of 1914–18. As a

Jew he was murdered by a group of Frei Korps officers, who also gave support to Hitler.

Auden's charade, a mixed bag of verse and prose, might be described as Opus 1, his reception into the literary world, his first work in his own idiom, which he recognised as such by continuing to publish it in his collected editions. It is a short, sharp dramatic piece exhibiting a blood feud in the North Country, recognisable Auden landscape with some of the verse in Wilfred Owen consonantal rhyme:

> Because I'm come it does not mean to hold
> An anniversary, think illness healed,
> As to renew the lease, consider costs
> Of derelict ironworks on deserted coasts.

This is the scenery he perversely preferred, Midlands machinery, especially if derelict, deserted factories and quarries, harsh limestone country.

The feud is between the Shaw and Nower families, the leader of the latter saying: 'On Cantley where a peregrine has nested, iced heather hurt the knuckles. Fell on the ball near time, the forward stopped.... These I remember, but not love till now. We cannot tell where we shall find it, though we all look for it till we do, and what others tell us is no use to us.' Here is already the authentic Auden.

The piece appeared when he was a prep-school master, and was dedicated to Day Lewis when he was another. Each side is engaged in shooting the other up, like gangs of schoolboys; I find my marginal comment at the time was, 'schoolboy stuff, a boy-scout world'. Reading it again years later I am reminded of Lorca's *Blood Wedding*, though I do not suppose that Wystan had come across Lorca at that time.

Later that year the piece featured in *Poems*, Auden's first Faber volume, with whom he was to publish for the rest of his life – a slim, elegant blue paperbacked booklet at half-a-crown. Those were the days! It was dedicated to Isherwood with a private joke for the initiated:

Let us honour if we can
The vertical man
Though we value none
But the horizontal one.

These oracular 'shorts', as he called them, were to be characteristic of
him: he wrote them throughout the rest of his life, not simply in the
last phase, as people think.

The important thing about this first little book is that in it Auden
thus early found his own Voice, and achieved his own style –
remarkable enough on any account. Already we encounter first lines
which immediately arrest the attention, of which brilliant examples
were to come.

Which of you waking early and watching daybreak break
Will not hasten in heart, handsome, aware of wonder . . .

There it all is, excitement expressed in the alliteration that comes
naturally, if mysteriously, to a true poet.

Here is another oracle, starting off a poem:

It is time for the destruction of error.

It is Auden laying down the law to his circle, and they were properly
impressed by it. But what does it mean? Has it any meaning, if one
pauses to consider? His claque took it from him, some of them – the
imitative Day Lewis, for example – taking over his language. Wystan
undoubtedly thought of himself as a leader (as I did):

From scars where kestrels hover,
The leader looking over
Into the happy valley . . .

This is the 'Paradise', as he described it to me years later in New
York, to which he could never go back – the country of lost youth,
those years when he had been happy, the early thirties. (Not so for
me: they were years of gathering ominousness, illness and pain
physical and mental, misery.)

The Auden themes are foreshadowed – the middle-class nostalgia for union with the working class, the workers in person:

> On Sunday walks
> Past the shut gates of works
> The conquerors come
> And are handsome.

Freud is present behind the scenes, though one hardly needs a Freud to interpret it. The Berlin boys are there:

> ... always with success of others for comparison,
> The happiness, for instance, of my friend Kurt Groote,
> Absence of fear in Gerhart Meyer
> From the sea, the truly strong man.

Admiration is for male qualities:

> But standing now I see
> The diver's brilliant bow,
> His quiet break from the sea,
> With one trained movement throw
> The hair from his forehead, [etc.]

This could speak for the handsome Gabriel Carritt, whose family of brilliant boys were the sons of E.F. Carritt, philosophy don at University College, across the street from All Souls.

Wystan's chosen background was not the Oxford I loved – I had had enough, like D.H. Lawrence, of working-class squalor all my youth – but industrial England. Much of the unemployment of the thirties was needless then, for the country had not let itself in for insane importation of surplus population into an overcrowded island:

> Smokeless chimneys, damaged bridges, rotting
>   wharves and choked canals,
> Tramlines buckled, smashed trucks lying on
>   their sides across the rails;

> Power-stations locked, deserted, since they drew
> the boiler fires;
> Pylons fallen or subsiding, trailing dead
> high-tension wires ...

Next Spender took up the pylons into his poetry. Such was the force of Wystan's personality, and his influence on his friends. (Not however on Betjeman or me – with me the earlier Eliot was everything: defeat, disillusionment, despair. Not even religion to go to.)

However, Eliot – nursing father to us all – recognised a new and original voice, and wrote of Auden with more enthusiasm than for anyone else as 'one of the few poets of first-rate ability who have so far appeared to voice the post-war generation, a generation which has its own problems and its profound difficulties'. Wystan did not express them for me: I was much more in tune with the Oxonian spirit of Betjeman, traditional and nostalgic. Eliot paid tribute to Auden's 'exploration of new form and rhythm', and recognised the excitement of 'the unfamiliar metric and the violent imagination.' He admitted the obscurity, having often been himself charged with being obscure. I never found Eliot obscure, and I do not like obscurity in either prose or verse. Neither did Betjeman: he disliked Browning and opted for Tennyson. So do I.

Two years later Faber published *The Orators: An English Study*. With it the recognisable voice of Eliot announced, 'It is only within the last few years that it has been possible to distinguish the existence of true growth among the youngest of our poets. Believing that it is a matter of importance to make their work available not to collectors only but to as wide a public as may be found, we have devised a format which is both convenient and cheap. Such titles as are chosen will, it is hoped, prove to be representative of the best work of coming men.' Auden was pointed out as the coming man. He was born under a lucky star, and indeed had luck with him all the way along – the *luck* that is necessary if a man is to leave a name in history or literature. This Eliot had too, on a scale which, as I know, he never expected.

The Orators, 1932, was another *Vermischung* of prose and verse, mostly prose with six 'Odes' at the end. Eliot described it as 'not a collection but a single work with one theme and purpose.' I fail to see the single theme or purpose: what unity it has is in its authentic Auden idiom, its contemporary tone, characteristics, references and private jokes for the group. Dedicated to Spender, it is a notebook of clever schoolboy pieces and jottings. Indeed it begins with an 'Address for a Prize-Day', a parody of such things which incorporates an actual slab of such a speech delivered by the headmaster of the prep school where Wystan was teaching. The tone throughout is a schoolmaster's talking oracularly, if obscurely, to pupils. Confirmed by Eliot, it was received with awe. Auden later condemned it candidly: 'A fair notion fatally injured.' 'A Communist to Others' – what *naiveté*! – their only excuse that they were young and didn't know what they were playing with.

I regarded it as middle-class posturing – ludicrous in the poetry of Day Lewis, later a Labour appointment as Poet Laureate:

> Revolution, revolution
> Is the one correct solution –
> We've found it and we know it's bound to win.

Or,

> Yes, why do we all,
> Seeing a Red, feel small?

A middle-class feeling of inferiority which I did not share; nor, an activist in the Labour Movement, did I write such naïve nonsense in my own verse.

One sees that a main aim was to *épater le bourgeois*. One jotting runs: 'Fourth Day. All menstruation ceases. Vampires are common in the neighbourhood of the Cathedral, epidemics of lupus, halitosis, and superfluous hair.' Another day registers: 'What have I written? Thoughts suitable to a sanatorium' – a school sanatorium, I suppose. Anyhow, I was not a *bourgeois*, and I was not impressed.

They were middle-class rebels, in revolt against their class and upbringing. This made a great difference between them and me: I was not one of them, though friendly to them and helped to promote them – after all, we were all on the Left, with common targets and objectives. I observed them from the sidelines. Actually, *they* were on the sidelines; I was in the thick of the Labour Movement, an active Party candidate all through that hopeless decade.

Anyone on the margin of the group can recognise the names and private references. In addition to the sainted Three there are Day Lewis, Edward Upward, Rex Warner, all prep-school masters; then Gabriel Carritt, Captain of Sedbergh School XV, Dick Crossman, 'a rather dirty Wykehamist' of Betjeman's poetic description. There are the favourite schoolboy clichés: 'Execution of a spy in the nettled patch at the back of the byre.' Or again, the half-baked prejudices and complexes: 'From all opinions and personal ties; from pity and shame; and from the wish to instruct us, O Sexton Blake, deliver us.'

Instead of instructing others, they could have done with a good deal of instruction – about politics, for example. The only way to be effective on the Left in Britain, if at all, was to join the Labour Party, or at least link up with it, not the CP or ILP. Auden's biographers make the point, quite rightly, that he was not really political, did not understand politics. At the time of the General Strike in 1926 (I was in hospital, with peritonitis), Wystan said blithely that he didn't think anybody took the General Strike seriously! It was a very serious matter indeed, both for the Labour Movement and the country.

Among the group's Enemies listed appears 'the Oxford Don: "I don't feel quite happy about pleasure."' We shall see that he had a point. Of the Enemy:

> His collar was spotless; he talked very well,
> He spoke of our homes and duty and we fell.

Among enemy occupations were collecting and talking to animals; a sign of an enemy house was old furniture. Very well, I was already given to collecting old furniture – not perhaps appropriately for a horny-handed son of toil, but I had had enough of a working-class home, without books, pictures, taste; and I have always been fond of talking to animals.

Beethameer is named as an enemy:

> Beethameer, Beethameer, bully of Britain,
> With your face as fat as a farmer's bum ...
> In kitchen, in cupboard, in club-room, in mews,
> In palace, in privy, your paper we meet
> Nagging at our nostrils with its nasty news ...

Beaverbrook was fair game, with his regular support of Appeasement, his assurance through all his newspapers at New Year 1939: 'There will be no war this year.' Even so, Evelyn Waugh – who never had any use for Auden or respect for the group – has a far funnier portrait of the potentate as Lord Copper.

Christ Church appears, with Roy Harrod, our economics don, and the Essay Club, of which Wystan was an unenthusiastic member. An enthusiastic one, I had been chairman; my first booklet, *On History*, arose out of discussions there, which I took seriously: it had been read as a paper to it in its original form. Then there is Dick Crossman, a close friend of Wystan's, to say no more:

> The week the Labour Cabinet resigned
> Dick had returned from Germany in love.

He had gone over to the girls and returned with an unappetising bride from Berlin. She eventually left him; but I remember eating a meal with them, squalidly in the kitchen, in the Barn they inhabited in New College Lane, round the corner from All Souls, the domestic life of which I much preferred.

Here was another German association of the group. The clue to Crossman – Maurice Bowra always called him 'Double-Crossman' – was that he had a German grandmother, after whom he took. A great, blond, blue-eyed Nordic, he was a dynamo of energy, charging away with no real sense of direction, all over the place. In these years he argued with me that the Nazis, National Socialists, were socialists, and shouted at Univ. high table (Clem Attlee's old college) that at least Hitler was 'sincere'.

In Berlin an awkward accident had befallen Wystan – his biographers describe it politely as a 'rectal fissure' – which he is candid enough to describe in 'Letter to a Wound'.

Looking back now to the time before I lost my 'health' – was that really only last February? Over and over again in the early days you showed your resentment by a sudden bout of pain. . . . I think I've learned my lesson now. Thank you, my dear. I'll try my hardest not to let you down again. Do you realise we have been together now for almost a year? . . . The examination on the hard leather couch under the brilliant light was soon over. Washing again as I dressed he said nothing. Then reaching for a towel turned, 'I'm afraid', he said. . . . You are so quiet these days that I get quite nervous, remove the dressing. No I am safe, you are still there. . . . Better burn this.

But he did not: he published it. His 'obscurity' stood in good stead: I don't suppose most of his readers understood what he was talking about – I certainly didn't. His 'wound' gave Wystan trouble for years – though nothing like so much as my duodenal trouble, and operations, gave me.

In the Odes the experience, dreams, visions, persons are brought together:

> Shaped me a Lent scene first, a bed, hard, surgical,
>   And a wound hurting;
> The hour in the night when Lawrence died and I came
>   Round from the morphia.

(I had had a queer experience when I heard of D.H.'s death: I thought I saw his 'Ship of Death' crossing our bay at home.) Here was Wystan's background: he

> Heard a voice saying, 'Wystan, Stephen, Christopher,
>   all of you,
>   Read of your losses' . . .
> And Stephen signalled from the sand dunes like a
>   wooden madman
>   'Destroy this temple' . . .

Christopher stood, his face grown lined with wincing
In front of ignorance – 'Tell the English', he shivered
              'Man is a spirit' . . .
Gritting his teeth after breakfast, the Headmaster
                              muttered
              'Call no man happy.'

The penultimate Ode is addressed 'To my Pupils':

Though aware of our rank and alert to obey orders,
Watching with binoculars the movement of the grass
                              for an ambush,
The pistol cocked, the code-word committed to memory . . .

It is still the schoolboy world, from which he has not yet emerged.
Nor is the work adult – difficult to understand why people should
have been impressed. I think it was the undertone of insecurity, of
obscure menace, as yet undefined, though it soon would be.
Moreover, he spoke to his generation, the schoolboys and undergraduates, many of whom would be, before many years were out, its
victims.

At New Year 1933 Hitler came to power. I had my own close
contacts with Germany, which were more serious and altogether
more significant than the frivolous ones of Auden, Isherwood and
co., notably through my friendship with Adam von Trott. I have told
some of the story of that in *A Cornishman Abroad*, for I have
preserved all his letters to me – mine to him were destroyed. It was a
highly emotional affair, all the more intense for being platonic;
though it made me deeply unhappy, I ought to be grateful, for it gave
me a window into the German soul. The end of the Weimar
Republic, the political circumstances, were enough to make one
miserable in themselves. The German working-class movement was
divided from top to bottom between Social Democrats and Communists; and, as if that were not enough, in the last year of the Republic
the Communists combined with the Nazis against the Social
Democrats, in the Berlin Tram Strike.

It was lunatic of course. Yet my Communist friend, Ralph Fox, would argue endlessly with me, defending the official Communist line that Social Democrats were 'Social Fascists'! All these people got what they so richly asked for from Hitler – Ralph eventually met his death in Spain. Why, why, wouldn't they see sense in time? I was distracted with anxiety, maddened by the idiocy of my own side. I had read *Mein Kampf*, and knew that Hitler would stop at nothing: once he had got his hands on power, he would never let go. He knew all about power, what politics are about; the ineffectives of the Left everywhere, in Britain and in Germany, in France and Spain, had no idea of power, or how to govern. And the fools underestimated Hitler. *Ich nicht*: I wrote at once to Adam, 'You can roll up the map of Europe.' (Pitt after Austerlitz.)

I meant that he might as well give up, there was no point in going on. I suggested that he might give himself up to historical research, and write a parallel to Burckhardt's classic on the Italian Renaissance with a book on the Renaissance in Northern Europe. Fortunately I was carrying on with my historical research, which helped to preserve one's sanity, though a heavy burden with teaching, writing *and* politics. In the end, research and writing prevailed – and I came to share Burckhardt's despair of politics, retreat and withdrawal into the inner life of the mind.

In this same year, 1933, Auden brought out *The Dance of Death*, which represented an active approach to the theatre, brought about by his old school-friend, Robert Medley's introduction to Rupert Doone the producer. To these two the piece – mostly verse with some prose – is dedicated. Eliot wrote of it with circumspection, 'Satirical in character, it will extend the reputation of its author, who is already recognised as "one of the four or five living poets worth quarrelling about".' A novel feature was the mingling of the performers on the stage with those coming up from the auditorium. I think Auden got the idea from Brecht.

The subject is given out by an Announcer: 'We present to you this evening a picture of the decline of a class, of how its members dream of a new life, but secretly desire the old, for there is death inside them.' It was Wystan's middle class that was supposed to be dying. Myself, I did not, and do not, feel involved. I was involved in doing

my best for the working class, and urging its interests. If it did not
know its own best interests – as it showed all the way along that it did
not – I had a retreat: I could always withdraw into historical research
and writing, All Souls, country life in Cornwall, America.

> The first scene informs us
> Europe's in a hole
> Millions on the dole –

Hitler had a remedy for that: smashing the Trade Unions and ending
unemployment by re-arming night and day for the conquest of
Europe.

Auden invites us to come out into the sun:

> We shall build tomorrow
> A new clean town
> With no more sorrow
> Where lovely people walk up and down.
> We shall all be strong
> We shall all be young, [etc.]

Some hopes! Working people hadn't even the sense to vote for
themselves – which was all I was urging them to do. In Germany they
voted in millions for Hitler, surprised when it led them into war; in
Britain they voted for Chamberlain's appeasing him, surprised that
it led them into war. Hitler knew to his fingertips what idiots the
masses are; the epigraph to *Mein Kampf* read, 'Germans have no
idea of the extent to which they have to be gulled in order to be led.'
This piece of candour was deleted on his coming to power.

The next section celebrates, typically, male beauty:

> He's marvellous
> He's Greek
> When I see him
> My legs go weak.

Those in the know would recognise the camp significance of 'Greek',
though something of Wystan's caution, or doubt, appears in

Some of you think he loves you. He is leading you on.

In a prose speech the Announcer instructs us that 'we must have a revolution, though all this talk about class war won't get us anywhere. . . . We must have an English revolution suited to English conditions, a revolution not to put one class on top but to abolish class.' The Chorus responds:

> The English revolution
> Is the only solution
> We take a resolution
> To follow thee.

Several scenes later it turns out that this settles nothing. 'He who would prove / The Primal love / Must leave behind / All love of his kind /'

> And fly alone
> To the Alone.

Apparently Auden had difficulty in reaching a conclusion to the problem he had set himself, and brought in Karl Marx as a *deus ex machina* at the end. Accompanied by two young communists, as it might be acolytes, Marx announces: 'The instruments of production have been too much for him. He is liquidated.'

So was the piece: it had no success: it did not deserve to have.

For the three years 1932–5 Auden was a prep-school master at Colwall, and very successful at it: he hadn't ceased to be a boy himself, was much in tune with them and good at putting himself across. One sees this reflected in his work, but it naturally increased the didactic, laying-down-the-law tone. That was no disadvantage in his American career, where it was widely accepted: the schoolmastering proved a useful apprenticeship. Meanwhile, 1934 saw the first publication of both his and Spender's *Poems* over there. The reviews generally preferred Stephen, and Yale thought him the better poet.

Stephen had a genuinely lyrical early gift, which petered out as he became a literary figure. I had an exchange of letters with him at this time – I had seen something of him at Oxford, gangling and blushing and bleeding at the nose; after he went down he brought handsome Tony Hyndman, his Welsh Guardsman friend, to tea with me in my old dark-panelled rooms in college.

The letters revealed a disagreement in opinion. With my view of poetry I thought that one should write as one deeply felt, since it arises from the deepest sources within one; and that might well be in conflict with one's intellectual stance. Stephen contradicted this: he considered that one should write one's poetry as and what one *thought*. This was in accordance with Wystan's life-long practice of writing poetry as an act of will. This, however, was contrary to the very nature of poetry: no wonder their poetry eventually dried up in them.

For myself, I did not write poetry unless emotionally moved to it; and what I deeply felt was in conflict with my Leftist intellectual position, i.e. what I thought. This may be illustrated from my attitude at the time. I admired Roy Campbell's poetry, such fine poems as 'Tristan da Cunha' and 'Horses on the Camargue'; but he was a Fascist. Never mind: I suggested him to Eliot, who took him up and Faber published him. Later, I came to his defence in the columns of Joe Ackerley's *Listener* – which published poems of mine. Campbell was astonished and, when I appeared at the BBC, thought to take me out for an evening's pub-crawl. He was disappointed at my reaction to that – a life-long member of the Duodenal Club! – and I never saw him again. He was not at all my cup of tea, but he was a fine poet.

Meanwhile, Wystan was writing *The Dog Beneath the Skin* with Isherwood, and when it was performed by their Theatre Group I dutifully went to see it. I was both impressed and puzzled, though the camp significance of the name of the village, where the action begins and ends – Pressan *Ambo* – was not lost on me, naughty boys. Once more, a *Vermischung* of prose and verse, the prose mostly Isherwood, the verse Wystan's, the play was subsequently much revised.

Today I regard it as immensely talented, and underestimated. It is too full of a number of things, and needs cutting down; but I find the whole of the first Act brilliant, it comes off. Vivacious and youthful, of course, very anxious to be up-to-date and 'with it', as 'it' was then. Drugging, for instance, comes in; there has been much progress in that field since then. Act II has a scene in a lunatic asylum, appropriately enough, which guys the idea of the Leader. Oswald Mosley was putting himself forward as such at the time, and went to Hitler's footstool for confirmation and blessing. Hitler did not think that he would make it, but for consolation witnessed Mosley's marriage to Unity Mitford's sister, blue-eyed, starry-eyed Diana.

The contemporary situation reveals itself in Wystan's choruses, his signature tunes:

> I see barns falling, fences broken,
> Pastures not ploughland, weeds not wheat.
> The great houses remain but only half are inhabited,
> Dusty the gunrooms and the stable clocks stationary.
> Some have been turned into prep-schools, [etc.]

We have made much further progress in that direction since. There is the Auden tone of menace, disturbing then, and all too prophetically fulfilled:

> The sky is darkening like a stain,
> Something is going to fall like rain
>   And it won't be flowers.

An echo from the First German War points to the Second. A woman villager expresses hatred of the Germans for what they had done (like Kipling's Mary Postgate):

> I had two sons as tall as you:
> A German sniper shot them both.

At the end she suddenly appears to address the village lads: 'Wave your dummy rifles about. It's only play now. But soon they'll give you real rifles. You'll learn to shoot. You'll learn to kill whoever they tell you to. And you'll be trained to let yourselves be killed too.'

It *was* disturbing to hear from the stage, to those of us who knew what Hitler's Germany portended. England would take no notice, just turned over in its sleep: no lead from the paralytic old men of the 'National' government. The sad thing was that Wystan had a real love of England:

> Wherever your heart directs you most longingly
>   to look; you are loving towards it:
> Whether north to Scots Gap and Bellingham
>   where the black rains defy the panting engine:
> Or west to the Welsh Marches; to the lilting speech
>   and the magicians' faces.

I never find myself going down the Hampshire valley towards Winchester, or approaching Salisbury with the marvellous apparition of the spire at end, without thinking of Wystan's line,

> . . . the cathedral towns in their wide feminine valleys.

Such is the power of a line of poetry to implant itself in heart and mind.

The oracular becomes familiar. 'Beware of those with no obvious vices; of the chaste, the non-smoker and -drinker; the vegetarian.' This might be me, I reflect; but could reply that one should keep one's vices to oneself, not flaunt them in public. Contemporary touches: even Virginia Woolf receives a touch:

> Do not speak of a change of heart – meaning five
>   hundred a year and a room of one's own –

which she had demanded in order to write. As against that we hear

> the sigh of the most numerous and the most poor.

I was sufficiently impressed by that line to adopt it into one of my own poems – though really I hadn't that middle-class sentiment about the poor, for I belonged to them. I shared Bernard Shaw's view that it was up to them to better themselves; but was finding more and more that they hadn't the sense to see or vote for their own interests:

> The General Public has no notion
> of what's behind the scenes.
> They vote at times with some emotion
> But don't know what it means.

We need not concern ourselves with the story of the play, good as it is. It all started with an earlier idea of Wystan's for a play, *The Chase*. The chase is after the lost squire of Pressan Ambo, who when found is to return to his inheritance and marry his sister. He turns out to be the Dog who accompanies the pursuers across the varied, mad scenes of Europe. When they return and he discovers himself, he rejects his inheritance for freedom and goes off with the boys.

In June of this year Wystan married Thomas Mann's daughter, Erika. This gave me a slight shock. It was an act of generosity on his part, to give her the necessary status to take refuge in this country from the Nazis. But wasn't it an act of bravado too? There was no question of making it a real marriage – wasn't that rather flaunting in the face of opinion? I was astonished that anyone could be so certain what his tastes were that he could take such a decisive step, prejudging the future. He was lucky as usual; it did him no damage, and he entered, if on a friendly, non-committal basis, that distinguished, but rather ghastly, family.

I had not forgotten Thomas Mann's earlier record, the author of *Reden eines Unpolitischen*, the book in which he aligned himself with German Irrationalism, the deep and the profound, against the superficiality of French Rationalism and British Empiricism, democracy and representative government, Western culture. Here was an apologist for the German disease, the German mind. He was now at liberty to repent, and take refuge in America, where he was received with open arms at his own portentous valuation. I have no patience with the over-inflation of his sentimental little story, 'Death in Venice', nor with Britten's wasting his genius on it, we all know why. In Wystan's biographies we are treated to a photograph of the humourless great man, towering over the family assembled at his feet.

In 1935 Mussolini put his foot through the international system, peace and security, with his attack on Abyssinia. He could and should have been stopped. The British government made a feint at stopping him through the League of Nations, but went on allowing supplies of oil for his campaign. The Labour Party patriotically supported the government – which took the opportunity to force a snap election, and catch Labour out a second time with a fraud. The old men were home with a large majority for the rest of the decade. Hitler drew his own conclusions and next year militarised the Rhineland. 'What is it to do with us? It's his own back door', argued the Editor of *The Times* against stopping him early in his tracks. A ship sunk in the Suez Canal, then under our control, would have stopped Mussolini. The British Foreign Secretary: 'But it would mean that Mussolini would fall!' The old men played the game of the dictators to eventual disaster, and the ruin of their country – 'a dishonest decade', indeed: Auden was right.

While I was fighting a second election in these discreditable, sickening circumstances, Wystan had six months' successful experience with an experimental film unit. With his extraordinary facility he rapidly wrote the text for two films, *Coal Face* and *Night Mail*, for which the young Benjamin Britten composed the music. This was the beginning of their friendship with its creative results.

Auden and Isherwood's next dramatic effort, *The Ascent of F6*, may have owed something to the film experience, for it is more tightly constructed, more concise, a successful play. I attended the first production loyally, and was duly impressed: this work spoke to me and for me. I find my first edition of it marked with comments, which have the interest of recording my reaction to it at the time.

Eliot thought better of it, and wrote: 'Some of the critics of *The Dog Beneath the Skin* thought that it was better to read than to see performed; others thought exactly the reverse: from this it is to be inferred that the play ought to be both read and seen.' (Clever Eliot – no catching him out; Wyndham Lewis to me: 'He is so sly, so *sly*.') 'It is concerned with the colonial rivalry of those great powers, Britain and Ostnia, which brings about the tragedy of the ace of mountain climbers, Michael Ransome, in the struggle to ascend the hitherto unconquered mountain giant known as F6.'

One could hear echoes of Eliot's voice in the play. He had made his first experiment with theatre the year before with *The Rock*, a church pageant (one can hardly consider the C. of E. as a 'Rock'). The choruses brought home the triviality of ordinary secular life:

> Here were decent godless people:
> Their only monument the asphalt road
> And a thousand lost golf balls.

Next Eliot contemplated a play on the subject of Thomas Becket and asked me what he should read: I suggested Dean Stanley's *Historical Memorials of Canterbury Cathedral*, and the play comes out of that.

In *F6* one recognises Eliot's voice in the passages like 'He is the formless terror in the dream, the stooping shadow that withdraws itself as you wake in the half-dawn.' I wrote in the margin, 'Eliot again – *Murder in the Cathedral*.' Or, 'You have felt his presence in ... the choking apprehension that fills you unaccountably in the middle of the most intimate dinner party.' That is the Eliot of 'Prufrock'. Again, 'Most men long to be delivered from the terror of thinking and feeling for themselves.' Regular, pure Eliot – though we have had worse terrors than that to encounter since.

A passage declares: 'There are two lives: the life of action and glory, and the life of contemplation and knowledge.' My marginal note says, 'The theme of the play is here announced – it is the typical modern dilemma, the dilemma for us, particularly mine: Poetry versus Politics.' I cite these notes simply for their interest as a reaction to Auden at the time. When he went off to the Spanish Civil War it was in order to take part in some action. It was comparable to my motive in being so active in the Labour Movement, standing for Parliament, etc. By nature a writer and intellectual, I felt inadequate, that I ought to test myself in the realm of action – so, doggedly I held on, placing a double strain upon myself.

On Wystan's lines

For the Dragon has wasted the forest and set fire to the farm;
He has mutilated our sons in his terrible rages ...

I have an ingenuous comment: 'The God of our Age and Time – a Fiend'. Each year in the thirties gave one reason to think so; eventually I wrote of Hitler, 'The stars in their courses fought for him.' He would never have got away with it – overthrowing the Versailles settlement, then the Locarno Treaty, militarisation of the Rhineland, annexation of Austria, conquest of Czecho-Slovakia – and renewed the German war for the conquest of Europe, if he had not been faced by a lot of feeble old men in Britain, who positively aided him, half-and-half in collusion, as with Mussolini, then Franco. They ruined their country – it was agony enduring it, watching it come about, helplessly.

In the play my view of the European situation is corroborated. 'The powers which I represent,' says Ransome's brother (Ransome goes on to his death), 'stand unequivocally for peace. We have declared our willingness to conclude pacts of non-aggression with all of you.' Pacts of non-aggression with Hitler! – they played straight into his hands. The Anglo-German Naval Agreement of this year was the greatest folly: Hitler had no intention of abiding by it, but took advantage of it to build the biggest battleship afloat, the *Bismarck*, which was to sink the pride of the British fleet, the *Hood*. The speech in the play goes on, 'We now find ourselves in a position of inferiority which is intolerable to the honour and interests of a great power. We have constantly reiterated our desire for peace', etc. What was the use of that, talking to Germans? Hitler meant to renew the war and – faced with such folly – he achieved it in far more favourable circumstances than they had in 1914.

At the end of the play I find long notes summing it up as 'a myth of our time, as was *Murder in the Cathedral* – only where that turned away its face from a contemporary solution, which places it in the Reaction, with Auden and Isherwood the direction, the *end*, is of our time. It preaches stoicism of a rational kind, with which to face a world about which they have no illusions.' The comment reads innocently enough now, but it had its point then, and went on: 'The myth becomes more specific: one sees it in terms of politics, 1935–6: the lives of men sacrificed by the ineptitude, duplicity, hypocrisy, of British policy.'

For me disillusionment was seeping in, flowing in. When Auden writes,

> Treating the people as if they were pigeons, giving
> the crumbs and keeping the cake

the comment reads, 'Quite rightly, since they are fools.' When Michael Ransome says, 'Under I cannot tell how many of these green slate roofs, the stupid peasants are making their stupid children', that spoke for me: the comment reads, 'Certainly'. That has its message too for today: the population explosion everywhere at the basis of trouble. At that time I was writing a poem called 'Too Many People':

> They are the truly happy, the fortunate
> As they go by on their carts, the hearses
>   decked with flowers,
> The mourning coaches following them
> Keeping up a decent appearance of grief . . .

I really had Swift in mind. But there is a curious parallel – curious, because Swift was never an influence with Auden, as he was with me – in these lines in the play: 'Happy those run over in the street today or drowned at sea, or sure of death tomorrow from incurable diseases! They cannot be made a party to the general fiasco.' The comment here ran simply: 'Great Britain 1931, Germany, Austria, Spain.' It was the fiasco of all our hopes. For another Swiftian poem I wrote, which Eliot vetted and published, I took for title a phrase of Auden's, 'The Stricken Grove'.

July to September Auden spent in Iceland, a holiday from Europe. But he did run into the brother of the egregious Goering with a party there. They 'exchanged politenesses at breakfast. Rosenberg is coming too.' He was the 'philosopher' of the Nazi movement, expounder of their Aryan racial rubbish and Nordic cult. (This

nonsense, from Houston Stewart Chamberlain, had been translated
and adopted by the Mitfords' grandfather – a clue to what led two of
them along their fatuous course.) 'The Nazis have a theory that
Iceland is a cradle of the Germanic culture [*sic*].'

Wystan travelled in a bus with these asses, who talked incessantly
about the Aryan qualities of the Icelanders: 'Die Kinder sind so
reizend: schöne blonde Haare und blaue Augen. Ein echt Germanis-
cher Typus.' And so on. He qualified as Nordic, with his fair skin and
flaxen-coloured hair; his father was passionately devoted to Icelandic sagas and Northern mythology, and had brought his boy up
on them. 'I love the sagas,' he said, but his strong common sense told
him 'what a rotten society they describe, a society with only the
gangster virtues'. The Nazis were gangsters – what a tragedy that the
liberalism of the Weimar Republic, the ineffectiveness, the ineptitude
of its democratic parties, should have allowed them to win, and
wreck Europe – when a civilised Germany could have been the
keystone of the arch!

Wystan had been subsidised by Faber to write a travel book about
Iceland, and combined with Louis MacNeice in the undertaking. He
had luck with publishers from the first:

> I love my publishers and they love me,
> At least they paid a very handsome fee
> To send me here. I've never heard a grouse
> Either from Russell Square or Random House.

(24 Russell Square was the well-known address of Faber, with which
I was pretty familiar in Eliot's days.) *Letters from Iceland* is a rag-
bag of a book, not much of a travel book; its main interest is
autobiographical, rather paradoxically for one who had an *idée fixe*
against the personal in literature. This is much to our purpose here,
for it tells us a good deal about him, in an objective, no-nonsense
kind of way. He could not think of a way to tackle the job, until it
occurred to him to write a long discursive poem addressed to Byron,
rather like *Don Juan*, a haversack into which he could pack
everything.

He describes himself without fear or favour:

> My passport says I'm five feet and eleven.
> With hazel eyes and fair (it's tow-like) hair,
> That I was born in York in nineteen-seven . . .
>
> My name occurs in several of the Sagas . . .
> In fact I am the great big white barbarian,
> The Nordic type, the too too truly Aryan.

He used to tell me that the name Auden was synonymous with Odin; apparently he thought so, though it may have an Anglian rather than Norse derivation.

Both his grandfathers were Anglican clergymen, and I call that a more important clue. At the time Eliot was writing *The Family Reunion* he said to me, 'The longer I live the more I realise that one isn't just oneself, but the product of one's ancestors; I am the product of a line of half-a-dozen clerics, and half-a-dozen schoolmasters.' He became the clerical schoolmaster of the Anglo-Saxon world. In Wystan too the cleric mingled with the schoolmaster: hence the dogmatising, the moralising, in addition to the didactic.

The family was High Church; this came through his mother, who adored her youngest:

> I grow more like my mother every day.

It is quite clear that he was spoiled, by my working-class standards: hence the physical indiscipline. He developed good middle-class discipline about work – but O the untidiness, the scruffiness, the positive grubbiness, the aura and aroma of nicotined unwashedness! (Eliot's neat and well-groomed prissyness for me.) As a boy he was extraordinarily precocious, and this made him unpopular with everybody; characteristically, he doesn't seem to have minded, and took no notice. I find myself in agreement with his fling against Normality, 'goddess of bossy underlings':

> I hate the modern trick, to tell the truth,
> Of straightening out the kinks in the young mind.

A marginal note here recalls the arguments I used to have with

Lancelot Hogben at the London School of Economics. My sympathies were all in favour of the exceptional, even at the expense of neurosis, rather than reducing to the dead level of the average – which was (and, I suppose, is) the aim with the educationists in schools. I even went so far as to indulge a cult of illness – as if I hadn't enough already – to sharpen the mind, as it can.

Wystan tells us that his aim in youth was to be a mining engineer, no thought of poetry. Where I did not agree with him was in his tastes:

> Tramlines and slagheaps, pieces of machinery,
> That was, and still is, my ideal scenery.

I call that perverse, a middle-class fantasy, like his middle-class idealisation of the 'workers'. I had had too much of a strain to get away from the china-clay industry my father worked in: with a great price obtained I that freedom. Wystan's father was a doctor – and there was a good deal of the clinical in the son.

His parents had given him a good education at a congenial, not grand, public school, Gresham's School, Holt, where he was happy – none of the whining against their public school one finds contemporaneously in the contributors to Graham Greene's *Old School Tie*. It was there that he came to terms, with no fuss at all – surprisingly – with his own sexual nature and inclinations; and, no less decisively, received the sudden inspiration from a friend to write poetry. This was a turning point in his life; hitherto he had been all for science, and came up to Oxford with a natural science exhibition.

All sorts of touches recall the thirties: Eliot's damning Byron as 'an uninteresting mind' – one can hear the sniff; the prejudice against Elgar. I remember Michael Tippett telling me then how much he disliked him; I said, 'Wait until you've written anything half so good before saying that.' Iceland is described as 'unreal': 'This is an island and therefore unreal.' The word 'real' was a regular cliché with this group – Spender recurs to it again and again, as if clutching hold of security; I do not know what they meant by it, nor, I expect, did they. There are various youthful hit-or-miss judgments – in favour of the collective, the only thing one mustn't be is 'independent'. Another Leftist cliché of the thirties: 'I can't believe that the character of one nation is much different from that of another'. One has only to use one's eyes – and Wystan tells us himself that he was very short-sighted.

Letters from Iceland is made up of letters to friends, from both Auden and MacNeice. There they all are for us: Isherwood, Betjeman, Crossman, the Carritts, William Coldstream, who did a portrait of Wystan at this time – as later he did one of me that was destroyed in the Blitz, when he lost everything in his flat in London. The book ends with an amusing series of bequests to figures and institutions, public and private, friends and acquaintance:

> to the College of All Souls the game
> Of pleonasmus and tautology.

This was because John Sparrow had attacked the group's verse in a little lawyerly book on Modern poetry (I used to call him 'the lawyer in literature'). He was bequeathed 'a quarter of a pound of fudge'; Isaiah Berlin 'a saucer of milk' – milk for the cat; to Geoffrey Grigson

> A strop for his sharp tongue before he talks;
> Item, to John Betjeman (the most
> Remarkable man of his time in any position)
> We leave a Leander tie and Pugin's ghost
>
> And a box of crackers and St Pancras Station
> And the *Church of Ireland Gazette* and our confidence
> That he will be master of every situation.

MacNeice bequeathed to his old Marlborough friend, Anthony Blunt,

> A copy of Marx and £1000 a year
> And the picture of 'Love Locked Out' by Holman Hunt.

45

At the end of all,

> We leave their marvellous native tongue
> To Englishmen, and for our intelligent island pray
> That to her virtuous beauties by all poets sung
>
> She add at last an honest foreign policy.

That spoke for us all.

That autumn Wystan produced what I think, altogether, is his finest collection of poems, one of the best volumes of verse of the century. He did not like the title with which Eliot provided it, *Look, Stranger!*; for American publication he provided his own title, *On This Island*, which describes it better. For all through it there runs a patriotic note, of love for the English landscape in all its forms, if particularly the North Country and the West. 'Prologue' is one of his most moving poems, and its opening lines have always remained in my mind:

> O love, the interest itself in thoughtless Heaven,
> Make simpler daily the beating of man's heart; within,
> There in the ring where name and image meet,
>
> Inspire them with such a longing as will make his thought
> Alive like patterns a murmuration of starlings
> Rising in joy over wolds unwittingly weave;
>
> Here too on our little reef display your power,
> This fortress perched on the edge of the Atlantic scarp,
> The mole between all Europe and the exile-crowded sea;
>
> And make us as Newton was, who in his garden watching
> The apple falling towards England, became aware
> Between himself and her of an eternal tie.

I always make a first distinction between poetry that is inspired, and poetry that is not; this is inspired. There are whole poems, naturally short ones, and many passages that are inspired. With these Auden not only found himself but reached, thus early, the prime of his achievement. He never surpassed it, as Yeats and even Victor Hugo surpassed themselves in their old age – but that is exceedingly rare. On the other hand, it is unjust to regard Auden's later poetry – as it is fashionable to do, notably with Larkin – as showing 'catastrophic' decline. He was still capable of writing good verse: it is a mistake to make a rigid contrast between the two periods, English and American. *Facilis descensus.*

A few of the love poems are inspired from beginning to end, and achieve – what is so rare with him – perfection. He did not believe, with Housman, in *la poésie pure* – a reason why his poems will survive most of Auden's. Interestingly there are a couple of echoes of Housman in the book, and a stanza was inspired by Bridges' 'Whither, O splendid ship, with white sails crowding?' These were unfashionable admirations at the time, and show how independent-minded he was – though an historian knows how foolish fashions in criticism are.

Again I have always remembered the perfect poem:

> Fish in the unruffled lakes
> The swarming colours wear,
> Swans in the winter air
> A white perfection have,
> And the great lion walks
> Through his innocent grove;
> Lion, fish, and swan
> Act, and are gone
> Upon Time's toppling wave . . .
>
> Sighs for folly said and done
> Twist our narrow days;
> But I must bless, I must praise
> That you, my swan, who have
> All gifts that to the swan
> Impulsive Nature gave,
> The majesty and pride,
> Last night should add
> Your voluntary love.

I could add a technical analysis of that perfect poem, but I do not propose to do it: I have not much use for the criticism of poetry, any more than Philip Larkin or John Betjeman had; the poem itself is the thing. We are pursuing Wystan, not literary criticism; he is present again, and in a more characteristic mood in the neighbouring poem – alas, an unhappy, unsatisfied one, far more frequent with him.

> Dear, though the night is gone,
> The dream still haunts today
> That brought us to a room,
> Cavernous, lofty as
> A railway terminus,
> And crowded in that gloom
> Were beds, and we in one
> In a far corner lay.

This is Berlin; I find a marginal comment that says 'Berlin never did any of them any good' – except, I suppose, that it provided Isherwood, Herr Issyvoo, with a best-seller. Then,

> Oh but what worm of guilt
> Or what malignant doubt
> Am I the victim of;
> That you then, unabashed,
> Did what I never wished,
> Confessed another love;
> And I, submissive, felt
> Unwanted and went out?

This was too often Wystan's fate – to be unloved; this theme comes up again and again in his poems, and all through his life. I think that this unslakeable desire must go back to his having been excessively loved by his neurotic mother. As D.H. Lawrence was; it inspired his best book, *Sons and Lovers* – and when she died, something broke in him. When Wystan's mother died, he was away from home, in exile in New York – and he came back to the Church of his childhood.

We may read this diagnosis clearly enough in

Language of moderation cannot hide;
My sea is empty and the waves are rough:
Gone from the map the shore where childhood played
Tight-fisted as a peasant, eating love.

In the same autobiographical poem depicting Christmas with the Carritts at 'the Hollies', we find him describing himself as

Son of a nurse and doctor, loaned a dream,
Your would-be lover who has never come
In the great bed at midnight to your arms.

That would be the handsome Gabriel in the big double bed there, provokingly alone. Fulfilled sex at this time was a matter of casual pick-ups. We can read:

That night when joy began
Our narrowest veins to flush
We waited for the flash
Of morning's levelled gun

where the sexual image is patent. Wystan felt no need to be apologetic: in a later essay he says, with markedly rational common sense, no one regrets a moment of pleasure. Plenty of these were available in Berlin:

. . . in the policed unlucky city
Lucky his bed.

No less in summer on Rügen Island, celebrated in Isherwood's prose and in Wystan's poem beginning with one of his striking first lines:

August for the people and their favourite islands.

There they all were, 'beside the undiscriminating sea':

Five summers pass and now we watch
The Baltic from a balcony: the word is love.

But was it – yet? I do not wish to criticise; but, when inspiration fails, lines are apt to be filled up with rhetorical statements: 'the band makes its tremendous statements', or 'the beautiful loneliness of the banks'. Or there is the thirties rhetoric about the workers:

> Brothers, who when the sirens roar
> From office, shop and factory pour
> 'Neath evening sky . . .

Still, there are moments, and poems, of pure inspiration, when he is by himself alone – when inspiration is apt to come:

> Out on the lawn I lie in bed,
> Vega conspicuous overhead
> In the windless night of June . . .

Passages now and then describe the English landscape unforgettably – no such descriptions of landscape, no such inspiration in the American poems:

As children in Chester look to Moel Fammau to decide
On picnics by the clearness or withdrawal of her treeless crown.

Altogether these early thirties were the time when Wystan was happiest and at his best as a poet. No such happiness for me: years of misery, public and private, increasing anxiety and pain.

While in Iceland Wystan heard of the outbreak of the Civil War in Spain, and was immediately anxious, as we all were. Here was the direct confrontation between the forces of evil – Franco, backed by Mussolini and Hitler, the dictators – against the legitimate Republic: the cause of democracy, social justice, liberal progress, was at stake. It has been usual since to think of it as the intellectuals' war, the Left intellectuals *par excellence* – naturally enough, for they flocked to the aid of the elected Republican government, attacked by the Army from Morocco, with its Moroccan levies, and the embattled Right. Among the recruits from the Left were young John Cornford, son of the poet Frances Cornford, Julian Bell, son of Clive Bell, the Bloomsbury art critic, and my friend Ralph Fox, already well known as writer and regular active member of the Communist Party. In fact he was already disillusioned, did not want to fight in Spain, and asked me to get him a job in Oxford. I tried his own old college, Magdalen, and again at All Souls: in vain. The CP, wanting martyrs, insisted on sending Ralph: he was shot down on the Cordoba Front, where the International Brigade was machine-gunned from the air by Italian planes. Hitler concentrated his for the evisceration of Guernica in the North (trial practice for Rotterdam later). Those three young Englishmen would have made a distinguished contribution, if they had lived.

All the intellectuals felt involved in the struggle – only Evelyn Waugh, as a die-hard Catholic, out on the Right. Eliot, cagey and clever as usual: 'While I am naturally sympathetic, I still feel convinced that it is best that at least a few men of letters should remain isolated.' This ultimately proved the best sense. Spender was already there to attend a conference of intellectuals in Madrid – his occupational disease (not good for poetry). Auden felt under the necessity to do something for the cause; his recruitment was made much of by the *Daily Worker*, good publicity: 'the most famous of the younger English poets and a leading figure in the anti-Fascist movement [was he?]. He will serve as an ambulance driver.'

Actually he saw very little of the war, and spent most of it in hotels in Barcelona and Valencia, where he met up with *gourmet* Connolly, and had 'a good lunch with much Perelada Tinto'. Many years later Auden said, 'I did not wish to talk about Spain when I returned because I was upset by many things I saw or heard about.' And no wonder: he was upset by the closing and burning of churches, the killing of priests and nuns on one side; answered by such atrocities as the shooting of Spain's most brilliant poet – Auden's opposite number – Lorca.

His letters are descriptive of what went on behind the Republican lines. 'Everywhere there are the People. They are here in corduroy breeches with pistols on their hip, in uniform, in civilian suits and berets. They are here, sleeping in the hotels, eating in the restaurants, in the cafés drinking and having their shoes cleaned . . . doing all those things that the gentry cannot believe will be properly done unless they are there to keep an eye on them.' (Nor are they: look at British railway stations today.) 'Once a man has tasted freedom he will not lightly give it up; freedom to choose for himself and to organise his life.' They are incapable of organising life in the mass – as the Russians well know.

Auden had no real understanding of politics, or he would have realised that the Republic was doomed to defeat, with the idiot working-class divided from top to bottom between Socialists and Anarchists, incapable of pulling together, with the Communists thrown in, eventually happily engaged in killing each other. When he returned he was tactful enough – he had the useful gift of tact – to lie low and say nothing; but he wrote a poem, *Spain*, which was published as a pamphlet and won much acclaim from the Left.

I do not think highly of it. It exemplifies his besetting sins of indirection, allusiveness, obscurity merging into meaninglessness. His biographer tells us that 'meaning was never Auden's greatest interest'. I call that his greatest defect, for what is writing for but to express and communicate? Almost the only stanza that comes through clearly is this:

> On that arid square, that fragment nipped off from hot
> Africa, soldered so crudely to inventive Europe,
>   On that tableland scored by rivers,
> Our fevers' menacing shapes are precise and alive.

And the repeated refrain is clear: 'But today the struggle'. The poem concludes with the much discussed lines,

> History to the defeated
> May say Alas but cannot help or pardon.

He came to disagree so violently with that conclusion that he scored it out in all the copies he came across and wrote, 'This is a lie', and eventually deleted the whole poem from his Works.

I do not know what is wrong with the statement. We had grievous reason to say 'Alas' and regret the defeat in Spain. The infamous 'National' government in Britain helped to defeat the Spanish

Republic with its 'Non-Intervention' policy, denying arms to the legitimate Spanish government, while our enemies, Mussolini and Hitler, poured in arms to the rebels and saw to its defeat. But the Left contributed to its own defeat by its hopeless incompetence, and the lack of governing sense, the sense of power, by which it was betraying good causes everywhere to the evil ones, who understood the facts of power and were all too effective. I was constantly urging this in Left papers (and was sometimes called 'Fascist', for being a realist). In fact, history does not pardon the defeated; neither do I.

Travelling in Spain, after Franco had won, I had a brief exchange with a couple of young Spaniards who had fought in the trenches before Madrid – or at least had been in them. They realised that the Republic had been 'no go', had virtually defeated itself. I had no sympathy with ineffectives in politics, who had no sense of power; being an active Labour man in those days, I used to put it to myself, was for ever 'building bricks without any straw'. When I came back from Franco's Spain I wrote that what Spain needed was less politics and more irrigation. It got that at least with Franco.

Some of that summer Wystan spent at Dover, where they were joined by the sainted *guru*, E.M. Forster, moral mentor of them all – I do not know whether accompanied by his policeman, his 'boy in blue', as he used to call him. Auden wrote a rather fine descriptive poem about that historic port of entry – I prefer his descriptive pieces to his rhetoric and abstract adjurations. I wish there were more of them; as time went on in America, and he became an international figure, there were more of the latter.

Here is Dover, with its tunnel through the chalk Downs, the ruined Roman pharos looking phallically over the harbour, the Norman castle floodlit at night, the Regency sea-front with its loiterers.

> Here live the experts on what the soldiers want,
> And who the travellers are

> High over France the full moon, cold and exciting
> Like one of those dangerous flatterers one meets and loves
> When one is very unhappy, returns the human stare . . .

The soldier guards the traveller who pays for the soldier . . .
Some of these people are happy.

It is a tell-tale poem. The couple otherwise occupied themselves with their last dramatic effort together, *On the Frontier*. This is the slightest of their joint efforts, and generally regarded as inferior to the others, though the faithful Group Theatre produced it that autumn. It is dedicated to Britten:

> The drums tap out sensational bulletins;
> Frantic the efforts of the violins
> To drown the song behind the guarded hill:
> The dancers do not listen; but they will.

This was the Auden note of menace in the thirties, authentic enough – and prophetic: it was fulfilled.

> Will people never stop killing each other?
> There is no place in the world
> For those who love.

Here is the other side of the Auden–Isherwood message: we might regard it as the private side, except that they made it so public. As such, I find the piece eaten out with sentimentality.

Next their ever-helpful publishers came up with a commission for a new travel book. In the Far East the Japanese were now putting their foot through the international system with their wanton war on an amorphous China. Wystan, who was not wanting in courage, opted for that, with Isherwood. The stage would not be crowded out with other intellectuals, competitive prima donnas: 'We'll have a war of our very own.'

They were given a great send-off. Grigson, who was making a career out of attacking Edith Sitwell and sucking up to Auden, devoted a double number of *New Verse* to celebrating him. He refused the original poetry of Betjeman as not being 'with it', and with pig-headed obstinacy always went on refusing to recognise it because, in John Piper's words, he had been wrong in the first place.

A grand literary party was given under the patronage of E.M.
Forster, with his barely adolescent *protégé*, Benjamin Britten, who
had set some of Wystan's cabaret songs, 'O tell me the truth about
love'. This has several recognisably demotic dirty touches:

> When it comes, will it come without warning
> Just as I'm picking my nose,
> Will it knock on my door in the morning
> Or tread in the bus on my toes,
> Will it come like a change in the weather,
> Will its greeting be courteous or bluff,
> Will it alter my life altogether?
> O tell me the truth about love.

When it came, it was with a knock on the door, and it did alter his
life, if not altogether.

The couple had an enjoyable time in China, keeping a travel diary
which forms most of their book, *Journey to a War*. At Chiang Kai-
shek's headquarters they had a typical encounter with a German
ADC, who gave them the news: 'Last night the German Army
marched into Austria. Of course it had to happen. And now I hope
that England and Germany will be friends. Austria was only causing
trouble between us. A good thing the whole thing is settled, once and
for all.' Typical German obtuseness; Austria was not the cause of the
trouble. This was Hitler's propaganda line, bemusing the British
with humbug about his pacific intentions; while privately he admitted later that he was afraid that all his peace-talk would undermine
his people's will to war. Meanwhile, Chamberlain, who had suc-
ceeded Baldwin at the helm of the drifting country, was bent on
'understanding' with Hitler and Mussolini, driving straight at last,
but on the rocks.

Another typical encounter was with an American lady missionary,
who button-holed Wystan: 'Are you *insured* with Jesus? Jesus has
positively *guaranteed* eternal life.' In Tokyo he was so shocked by a
screaming mob of robots seeing a troop train off that he dropped and
broke his spectacles. Such are idiot humans.

The book was dedicated to Forster, patron saint of them all:

> Though Italy and King's are far away,
> And Truth a subject only bombs discuss,
> Our ears unfriendly, still you speak to us,
> Insisting that the inner life can pay.

E.M. Forster's insistence on the inner life paid him very well; his retired residence at King's provided a model and an argument for Auden's later at Christ Church. A sonnet sequence ended the book, heavily revised later; but what is it about? Little is recognisable, except

> Think in this year what pleased the dancers best,
> When Austria died, when China was forsaken,
> Shanghai in flames, and Teruel re-taken . . .

America is addressed, asking Mankind: '*Do you love me as I love you?*' The terms are still relevant. A glimpse of actual scene is refreshing:

> Thin gardeners watched them pass and priced their shoes;
> A chauffeur waited, reading in the drive,
> For them to finish their exchange of views:
> It looked a picture of the way to live . . .

So thought our Christ Church contemporary, Harold Acton, who gives us a portrait of that vanished culture in *Peonies and Ponies*.

The *Commentary* in verse offers a fine summary of civilisation and the issues at stake. The Japanese 'even to themselves deny a human freedom':

> This is one sector and one movement of the general war
> Between the dead and the unborn . . .

> Never before was the Intelligence more fertile,
> The Heart more stunted . . .

> We wander on the earth, or err from bed to bed,
> *In search of home.*

That spoke for both of them, the need to find a home particularly for Auden.

The couple came back via the Pacific and the United States, which more than made up for any disappointments. They had a roaring reception in New York, popular celebrities to meet them, *Harper's Bazaar*, theatres, parties, bars, pick-ups. Wystan fell in love with New York, as all Englishmen do – after all, it is the most exciting city in the world, the greatest urban creation of modern man. On the way back to England he was out of spirits, depressed, and gave the cause that he could never find anyone to love him. The fact was that he was not very well equipped for love.

And yet, in Berlin their psychological mentor, John Layard, had fallen in love with him; when the younger couldn't respond, his senior shot himself on Wystan's doorstep. Layard recovered – though not a very good advertisement for his subject, supposed to be therapeutic. Matthew Arnold incurred some disapproval for his condemnation of the Shelley–Byron circle, and their goings-on: 'What a lot!' I do not condemn the Auden circle, but I preferred the sedate way of life, the lifestyle, of Eliot, sad as that was (and so was mine).

Maynard Keynes, who was a generous encourager of the arts and shared the group's liberal views about sex, paid for the production of *On the Frontier* at Cambridge, as he had done for that of *The Ascent of F6*. How lucky they were in their backers, publishers, and all – if not always in love! The promiscuous Cambridge Apostle, Guy Burgess, was not impressed by *On the Frontier*: 'The trouble about Wystan, Christopher and Stephen is that they haven't got the foggiest notion what politicians are really like.' My own judgment is, rather, that they did not know what *politics* really are.

And characteristic of the appalling thirties, when humbug and hypocrisy were in the ascendant, the stuff of British politics, was the Lord Chamberlain's insistence that Scandinavian names should be substituted in the play for the original German ones, in order not to offend Nazi susceptibilities. This was in keeping with the time, when the guilty editor of *The Times* could plead that he spent night after night keeping out of the paper anything that could offend them, and sacked his able Berlin correspondent, Ebbott, for reporting the truth about them and what they were up to. It was not merely sickening, it made one ill. The devoted Wigram within the Foreign Office, who realised perfectly what was happening and what it would lead to – and reported secretly to Churchill, equally well informed and alarmed – suffered a stroke and died. Vansittart, who was entirely right about the Germans and their intentions, was kicked out of the way for Cadogan, more amenable to Chamberlain and his pro-Hitler adviser, Horace Wilson.

Auden and Isherwood had for some time been planning to return to the States. At a Christmas party in Brussels Wystan greeted his pal:

> May your life in the States become better,
> May the shadow of grief disappear,
> But – God! – if you ever turn heter,
> I won't wish you a happy New Year.

Wystan's own young 'amant', Petit Jacques, is addressed:

> When the touch of your hand made me bristle,
> And your lips made me hot as a coal,
> Just after I learnt you could whistle –

a heterosexual accomplishment –

> And before I realised you stole.

A serious sonnet, 'Brussels in Winter', which a biographer oddly finds 'oddly persuasive', makes the point:

> And fifty francs will earn a stranger right
> To take the shuddering city in his arms.

In January 1939 the couple took off for America, the Master, the highly ethical Forster, seeing them off. On their way across, Isherwood realised: 'It just doesn't mean anything to me any more – the Popular Front, the Party line, the anti-Fascist struggle. I suppose they're OK . . . I simply cannot swallow another mouthful.'

'Neither can I,' said Auden.

The truth was, neither of them was really political, or understood politics. Or, by the same token, society.

We might conveniently sum up here the Auden–Isherwood partnership. Isherwood was three years senior, and Auden looked up to his critical intelligence as to no one else. Isherwood's biographer tells us that his early novel, *All the Conspirators* – for he was cast to be the novelist of the group –

> is an indictment of the Edwardian family in general and barely conceals its writer's personal vendetta against his own family in particular. *The Memorial* is an indictment of British society at large and sees even the threatening mother as herself a victim of a diseased civilisation. . . . That 'land you were once proud to own' . . . 'those handsome and diseased youngsters'.

A working-class man sees them merely as *spoiled* – Isherwood running away from the university when he himself had had such a struggle to get to one! 'It is the landscape of Auden's early poetry; it is also Upward's vision of doomed youth, during his holiday with Isherwood at Freshwater Bay in 1928.' (No such holiday for me!) 'It is a myth about the 1920s shared by the writers of the 1930s.' I did not share it. For myself I had, during these early years at All Souls, a more serious though secret cult of the young Fellows before me who had given their lives for their country in 1914–18.

For Isherwood, at school, whose own father had been killed, all he could see was 'dishonest cant about loyalty, selfishness, patriotism, playing the game and dishonouring the dead'. But was it cant? Was it dishonest? I find more cant in them. We learn that Bergmann in *Prater Violet* offers 'a subtle criticism of the fascist assumptions underlying British society in general.'

Enough of this nonsense! It will be seen why I am not much of an admirer of Isherwood, and regard the overestimation of him by all the media as gross and absurd. I do not deny his talent, a minor talent of our time, his real interest that of a pathological case centring upon himself, rather than of value as reflecting upon society in general.

Auden was a different matter, far more worthy of respect: it was time for the partnership to dissolve. Isherwood felt 'strangely alienated by New York', and sensibly realised that Auden was the 'dominant figure who was going to succeed there'.

3

New York

Auden and Isherwood received a grand welcome in New York, but parted on their separate ways; though remaining friendly, they did not cooperate in another work. Isherwood was bound for the colony of English expatriates in Los Angeles, pacifist by persuasion and dedicated to what Auden regarded, with his usual common sense, as Hindu 'mumbo-jumbo'. Their *guru* was Gerald Heard (of whom Hogben said to me, 'Gerald heard, but not understood.') Aldous Huxley, more intellectually respectable, was another. High-minded and spiritual to a degree, though not without a taste for the things of this world distinctly carnal in flavour, they were pacifists. Auden was not a pacifist; common sense again told him that that was not a practical proposition, not a viable political position, in this wicked world, with humans as they are.

Others of Auden's friends joined him in New York. Louis MacNeice did not stay the pace long, he found the life uncongenial; young Britten and his friend the tenor, Peter Pears, held out rather longer – Britten to collaborate with Auden in an American opera, *Paul Bunyan*, and various other works. Then their collaboration broke down – rather sadly, or we might have had musical genius married to a librettist worthy of it, something like Richard Strauss and Hugo von Hoffmannsthal – instead of the inferior stuff of *The Rape of Lucretia*, etc.

It is also clear that their friendship broke down – I can understand why. Artistic inspiration is a tender plant – so much so that it does not do with too much talky-talky about it. (A prime reason why the upas-tree of literary criticism is so inimical to creativeness.) It does not do to expose the seed from which art springs to the blaring light of critical discussion: it springs up in the dark, from deeper sources, the unconscious; the brainwork is the shaping instrument, not the source.

There was always too much talk around and about Auden, and the sensitive Britten, not yet sure of himself, found Wystan intellectually overbearing. Britten needed to find *himself*, not to be borne down by Wystan's schoolmasterly didacticism – which was to go down so wonderfully in American women's colleges. (Betjeman similarly wilted under C.S. Lewis's intellectual bullying.) Earlier in England Wystan was aware of this fault, and would ask why take what he said so seriously. America flattered him; never very critical of himself, this defect increased with him, unhumorously, deleteriously.

He fell at once into the ways of New York life and enjoyed it enormously – for many years, up until he began to feel the onset of age. This was immensely fortified by his finding love and companionship. I have noted all the way along this exorbitant, almost childish, need to be loved, and have put it down to his having been spoiled as a child. This is corroborated in a poem of just this time:

> For I, after all, am the Fortunate One,
> The Happy-Go-Lucky, the spoilt Third Son.

Just so.

America took him up in a big way; he was looked after from the first, with even more than the usual American generosity – for the new recruit was someone of major interest, vivacious and vital – not only by other writers, publishers, literary papers, schools, colleges, campuses, but by a host of acquaintance and a number of immediate friends he made. He had an obvious gift for friendship and, in spite of his uncouth ways, was always a gentleman; if not always polite, he had *politesse du coeur*. He responded to all this with immense verve; it needs no explanation that he was willing to become an American citizen. Any more than – the other way round – it needs any explaining that Henry James and Eliot chose to become English subjects. The world today is far too dangerous for any parochialism

within the English-speaking world. A nineteenth-century exile from
Russia said that its literature was his country. The far richer and
more marvellous literature in our language – contributed to by so
many streams, not only English-speaking countries, but notably
from India, for example – is our country. I do not think myself an
exile when in America (anyway most of the Cornish people are
there); neither did Wystan. I think of Henry James and Eliot, Auden
and Huxley, and even Isherwood as all helping to keep the Atlantic
bridges – perhaps even a 'special relationship' – going.

What was fundamental for Wystan was that he at last found love,
still more companionship, with Chester Kallman. I never once met
him, perhaps was not allowed to meet him, but Eliot's widow told
me that, when young, he was rather an Adonis, a blond with a mop
of fine hair. He also had other qualities: an excellent cook (I do not
underrate that), cultivated musically, naturally intelligent. They
owed much to each other: Wystan learned musically, Chester
learned to write, and became a good librettist alongside of the
Master.

> For now I have the answer from the face
> That never will go back into a book
> But asks for all my life, and is the Place
> Where all I touch is moved to an embrace.
> And there is no such thing as a vain look.

He had had enough of unrequited love:

> Like love we often weep
> Like love we seldom keep.

Now –

> Nowhere else could I have known
> Than, beloved, in your eyes
> What we have to learn,
> That we love ourselves alone.

This experience transcended self-love. When Wystan found later that Chester's feeling for him was affection, not love, he did not withdraw his own devotion: he remained constant and true and dedicated. He needed someone to love and look after, even to make sacrifices for – for Chester was not easy to live with, with his inconstancy, the endless casual affairs, the liking for roughs, who on one or two occasions roughed up the apartment. Once, when I was in New York, *Time* wanted to discuss with me a 'Profile' of Auden, but found, when they went into it, that the private life was too much for their chaste readers. With me Wystan was cagey about it; never mentioned Chester, nor was I bidden downtown to their squalid domesticity. I kept some contact, and Wystan would come all the way uptown to my modest hotel near Central Park. There he would imbibe a couple of his favourite drink, a 'Bloody Mary' – I can't tell one drink from another, so I forget what it is made of; while we talked about Oxford mostly, a great gossip, he always wanted news of our old acquaintance, tutors, etc.

The inevitable outbreak of war came with Hitler's attack on Poland, 1 September 1939. Was the war 'inevitable'? Churchill always thought not: he called it 'the unnecessary war'. He held that, if Hitler had been stood up to in time, he would not have got away with it. This would have necessitated coming to an understanding with Soviet Russia. Chamberlain and co. would never stand for this: they preferred an understanding with Hitler, Chamberlain expressly preferred 'to trust Herr Hitler's word'. All that 'Collective Security' meant in essence was keeping the cordon around Nazi Germany, so that the abscess would burst inside. I asked Hugh Dalton if the Labour Party could not reach an agreement with Churchill in time; he was not averse, for he realised the almighty danger, but answered, 'How many Tories could he bring over with him in the House of Commons? Only twenty, or at most twenty-five.' Such was that unspeakable assembly that led Britain to her ruin – her splendid historic record came to an end in flames in the heroic Churchillian years 1940–5.

When the war began – which the British upper classes brought down upon their country (they have paid for it) – Auden and his expatriate friends were attacked. I never attacked him. I have only one reservation to make here. I thought, and still think, that his poetry was the loser – and therewith our literature. His previous poetry had shown his patriotic feeling for England, his love of English landscape, particularly of the North Country. There is no knowing what sharing the experience of those heroic years would have inspired in him – we cannot tell. They were the most exciting years of one's life, what heights and depths, comradeship and suffering and endurance, anxiety and grief and pride – he missed it all. He was the loser.

I took no notice of the attacks on him – they came from the very people for whom I had no respect, the Appeasers themselves. One nasty epigram came from a third-rate Dean of St Paul's – a very inferior figure to the great, if gloomy, Dean Inge: 'To Certain Intellectuals Safe in America'. This unworthy cleric had exposed himself as a fervent Appeaser in the years before. Questions were asked in the House of Commons, the very assembly that had supported appeasing Hitler, Mussolini and Franco, the country's enemies, through thick and thin.

Very wisely Auden did not answer the attacks on him – as I should have done. He would not have known enough about politics to pinpoint these shoddy people's record. Again, I do not think he was as much upset by them as I should have been; he was not a Celt, and had a thick skin. Also, he didn't take notice of other people and their views overmuch. But he wrote some revealing Notes in his early days in New York. 'To be forced to be political is to be forced to lead a dual life.' (I had *forced* myself to be political, and the dual strain had nearly killed me.) 'Perhaps this would not matter if one could consciously keep them apart and know which was the real one. But to succeed at anything, one must believe in it, and only too often the false public life absorbs and destroys the genuine private life.'

This was very percipient of him: this was what it had very nearly done for me, at least the tension between the two had destroyed, for the time, both health and happiness.

In another Note he said: 'Artists and politicians would get along much better in a time of crisis like the present, if the latter would only realise that the political history of the world would have been the same if not a poem had been written, not a picture painted nor a bar of music composed.' This gave rise to much discussion, for it was the leader of the group, its most didactic voice, turning his back on the literature of engagement which they had all declaimed in the thirties. The boys had won much publicity by it. Now it was publicly disclaimed, and from self-chosen exile in New York. He had turned his back on the causes of the thirties. It was a very clean and clear cut – striking in its absoluteness, throwing off all old encumbrances and obligations. Naturally his former associates at home didn't like it, though they came to his defence. I could make no such clean cut – too many ties, too much involved emotionally – though I too had no further confidence in politics or political parties, social democracy or whatever: henceforth it was a struggle for survival, in 'a ruined century' (Auden's phrase) – and the historian well knows by whom.

Having cleared that issue out of the way – very important for what is called nowadays Auden's 'public image' – we may say, on the other side, that he needed new experience. His biographer emphasises that he was given to acting a rôle and was in need of a rôle to act. (This alone shows that he had not been so deeply *engagé* as I had been, or so profoundly disturbed by it all. He sloughed it off remarkably easily. The historian has never forgotten nor the Celt forgiven, any of it.) Auden was out to conquer a new world and, with everything aiding him, he did. But at a price.

The poems which he collected in *Another Time*, 1940, were mostly written before going to America, and keep up the standard of *Look, Stranger!*: the two are his best volumes. The new one contains a few American poems and is dedicated to Chester, so we may regard it as a summing-up of his English life and a bridge to the new. The poem he wrote from a dive on Fifty-second Street, the day Germany started her second war this century, indicts the country he had always favoured (tastelessly) against France:

> Accurate scholarship can
> Unearth the whole offence
> From Luther until now
> That has driven a culture mad . . .

My marginal note at the time simply says 'cf. my article, "What is

Wrong with the Germans".' This was in keeping, from an historian's point of view, with Santayana's philosophic diagnosis.[1]

The poem describes the landscape of New York:

> Into this neutral air
> Where blind skyscrapers use
> Their full height to proclaim
> The strength of Collective Man
> Each language pours in vain
> Competitive excuse

and the culture:

> Faces along the bar
> Cling to their average day:
> The lights must never go out,
> The music must always play,
> All the conventions conspire
> To make this fort assume
> The furniture of home.

We see that he is not yet at home; the lights of New York flash out ironically, when

> Our world in stupor lies ...
> May I, composed like them
> Of Eros and of dust,
> Beleaguered by the same
> Negation and despair,
> Show an affirming flame.

My one and only reproach to Wystan occurs in a marginal note here: 'From New York, it was not *chic*.' But perhaps that was, on reflection, unjustified. The affirmation he proclaimed became the most famous line he ever wrote:

---

[1] G. Santayana, *Egotism in German Philosophy*, 69.

We must love one another or die.

This was quoted as his message all round the literary world.[1] Once more it raised a doubt in his mind, and threw up a smoke-screen of dust. I do not fully understand why he objected to it so strongly; it is rhetorical, of course – there is too much rhetoric in this volume – and the absolute apposition is unconvincing, just not true: we *can* continue to exist without love. Auden tried emending it, but in the end cancelled the whole poem from his collected work. That is a pity, for it has historic interest at least.

One love poem in this book has one of his most moving stanzas:

> Lay your sleeping head, my love,
> Human on my faithless arm;
> Time and fevers burn away
> Individual beauty from
> Thoughtful children, and the grave
> Proves the child ephemeral:
> But in my arms till break of day
> Let the living creature lie,
> Mortal, guilty, but to me
> The entirely beautiful.

The theme of exile appears in 'Refugee Blues':

> Once we had a country and we thought it fair,
> Look in the atlas and you'll find it there:
> We cannot go there now, my dear, we cannot go there now.

Hitler and the German Jews appear in it, naturally, but the poem goes on too long – apt to be a fault with him at all times: he should have cut his work more rigorously – as Pound cut a mass of stuff out

---

[1] cf. the milksop Forster: 'He elicits a response which I cannot always explain. Because he once wrote "We must love one another or die", he can command me to follow him.' The response in his case is easy to explain.

of 'The Waste Land'. From a brief 'Epitaph on a Tyrant' he had
learned one thing from politics:

> He knew human folly like the back of his hand.

I had learned that too – but the hard way, most directly electioneer-
ing, *asking* the idiots to vote sense!

My crisp comment on 'the talkative city', Oxford, was the one
word: 'Fabricated'; and on the first stanza, 'No'. I did not like the
merely verbal trick,

> And the stones in that tower are utterly
> Satisfied still with their weight.

Too many tricks appear and are marked in my margins: the personi-
fication of abstracts – Edward Lear 'successfully reached his Regret';
inversions of sense and natural order, 'We are lived by powers we
pretend to understand' (are we?); 'the legions of cruel inquisitive
They', etc. Too frequent Auden signature lines: Edward Lear, 'a dirty
landscape painter who hated his nose'; A.E. Housman 'kept tears
like dirty postcards in a drawer'.

Sometimes the don in me was at issue with him over a point of fact.
In the excellent poem, 'Voltaire at Ferney', we read 'Dear Diderot
was dull but did his best.' No one who knew the author of 'Le Neveu
de Rameau' thought him dull: that connoisseur of men, Catherine
the Great, found him fascinating. And, laying down the law about
Matthew Arnold, Auden got him wrong:

> His gift knew what he was – a dark disordered city.

My comment says, 'No; inversion; phrase from Yeats.'

> And left him nothing but a jailor's voice and face,
> And all rang hollow, [etc.]

'Completely wrong, as about Tennyson', says the margin. Arnold
was nothing if not orderly, and nothing in him was hollow. As for

Tennyson, whom Wystan described as the 'stupidest' of poets – how undergraduate-silly; we now know how extraordinary and curious was the range of his reading, how odd was his humour in private, and how original his turn of mind. It is just silly, like Wystan's dismissal of *The Merry Wives of Windsor* as 'the worst of Shakespeare's plays': it is a rollicking, entirely successful farce. I dislike quick summary judgments in literature, art, or history – liable to be simply superficial.

The sonnet 'The Composer' is clearly Wystan's tribute to Britten:

> Only your notes are pure contraption,
> Only your song is an absolute gift.

This is contrasted with the poet fetching up images that 'hurt and connect'. 'Only connect' was a motto of *Guru* Forster, turned into a command of universal application by his claque – rather a joke when one thinks of his homo stories, not published till the moralist was safely under the sod. The theme of the sonnet is that music is amoral:

> You alone, alone, O imaginary song,
> Are unable to say an existence is wrong.

I do not know that this is so: one can detect the false, the vulgar, the insincere, the pompous, the brash, the brassy in music – to go no further than Strauss's *Heldenleben*, or *Sinfonia Domestica*.

The poem 'Herman Melville' has a camp reference to Billy Budd, about whom Britten was to write a boring opera – five Acts of all-male voices! Later he cut it down to two – but O what a bore, a whole evening of men's voices, without relief, when women's voices, or boys', are almost always more attractive and appealing.

Auden was more at home with psychiatrics than history, and for too long for his good; however, he sums Freud up fairly enough:

> . . . one who lived among enemies so long:
> If often he was wrong and at times absurd,
> To us he is no more a person
> Now but a whole climate of opinion.

That is no more than just; he was often wrong and absurd – I have never read a more absurd book than his *Moses and Monotheism*. But his *Weltanschauung* runs neck and neck with Marx – or has done – for a contemporary mythology.

I am more at home with Yeats, who – we are told in an Auden cliché – 'became his admirers'; and Time would pardon him for his views, as with Kipling's, for writing well. In my opinion Kipling's views require no pardon: he was roughly right about things, especially politics and modern society.

> In the nightmare of the dark
> All the dogs of Europe bark . . .

I found myself in agreement with Wystan about

> Intellectual disgrace
> Stares from every human face:

my note says, 'Q. for my Politics, etc.'

Next year, 1941, he produced a long discursive poem in the manner of the earlier 'Letter to Lord Byron'. This was no longer adolescent, but a mature poem revealing his exceptional power to conduct arguments in verse. It is in tetrameter, rhymed couplets; I regard it as a *tour de force*. In England the publishers gave it the title *New Year Letter*; Auden's own title for it was *The Double Man*, if that gives one any clue to its meaning for him.

It doesn't for me: I agree with Herbert Read, who was one of our *Criterion* group:

> He represents the modern intelligence in all its acuteness and confusion. His present misuse of a medium – misuse rather than abuse for it is a failure in communication – does not affect our faith in his genius, and our expectation of its eventual expression – either in verse that is 'simple, clear and gay' (his own demand), or in prose that is clear, simple and serious.

This is just and perceptive; we shall see how its forecast will work out.

I take my lead from Wystan, who tells us that he can but think in images. This is natural for a poet, and it ties in with my earlier diagnosis that he had sudden insights, often incisive and true, but that he lacked the capacity to *carry his thinking through*. The Eng. Lit. School at Oxford does not give that training; it is rare for it to produce a clinical work, like Iain McGilchrist's *Against Criticism*. Nor does Eng. Lit. anywhere seem to produce that kind of training – one reason why it cannot penetrate an Elizabethan historian's discoveries about Shakespeare, or even grasp their importance – 'irrelevant learning' declared one of its products, editing *The Times Literary Supplement*!

The thinking in the poem comes, then, in spurts – and a lot of it is sensible: I do not descry any long consistent argument as with Pope or Dr Johnson. It takes its departure from the cottage on Long Island belonging to Elizabeth Mayer – to whom the poem is dedicated – who welcomed there Wystan, Britten and Pears. So they had a lot of music, one of Buxtehude's passacaglias making a *civitas* of sound:

> For art had set in order sense
> And feeling and intelligence,
> And from its ideal order grew
> Our local understanding too.

Contrast the madhouse to which the Germans had reduced Europe:

> The grand apocalyptic dream
> In which the persecutors scream
> As on the evil Aryan lives
> Descends the night of the long knives.

That refers to the murders of June 1934, quite early on in Hitler's rule, when he murdered his closest friend Röhm, and some hundreds of opponents within and without the Nazi Party. The official total of deaths was some 1,250. Hitler was publicly thanked by the old hero of the first German war, the senile Hindenburg, the mass of the German people rallied behind the murderer.

And not a German can be proud
Of what his apathy allowed.

As for the English, whom not even this alerted:

Upon each English conscience lie
Two decades of hypocrisy.

True enough: ours were sins of omission, theirs were sins of commission. Plenty of humbugs afterwards, like the Nonconformist historian, Butterfield, made the plea that we were all equally to blame: pure humbug – we did not commit the murders. And the Night of the Long Knives was only the beginning: it is estimated that Hitler's rule executed some 25,000 of his own good Germans, apart from the millions of victims from the war and the extermination camps.

Auden understood well that this was the consequence of

What none before dared say aloud,
The metaphysics of the Crowd . . .
The hitherto unconscious creed
Of little men who half succeed.

I do not think he had enough historical and philosophical reading to know that it was also the consequence of what the Germans thought and taught for the past century, reduced to the terms of mass civilisation in which Hitler was a master. It is all there in *Mein Kampf*; I don't suppose Wystan had read it, neither had any of the responsible (!) British political figures who had dealings with him.

Auden's first home in New York was in Brooklyn:

Across East River in the night
Manhattan is ablaze with light.
No shadow dares to criticise
The popular festivities,
Hard liquor causes everywhere
A general *détente* . . .

Not with me, I may say. In Elizabeth Mayer's hospitable house they had Schubert and Mozart and Gluck, food and friendship.

> Our privileged community
> That real republic which must be
> The state all politicians claim,
> Even the worst, to be their aim.

He still makes obeisance to the ideal of building the 'Just City', a notion which the facts everywhere made irrelevant, and which I regarded as nonsense. Wystan himself realised that

> Our road
> Gets worse and we seem altogether
> Lost as our theories...

All that he was left with was

> ... true democracy begins
> With free confession of our sins.

I was left with not even that – no illusions about democracy.
   We are given a *tour d'horizon* of the United States, a rapid summing up of

> That culture that had worshipped no
> Virgin before the dynamo,
> Held no Nicea nor Canossa,
> *Hat keine verfallenen Schlösser,*
> *Keine Basalte,*[1] the great Rome
> To all who lost or hated home.

Did it not add up to much the same as my own poem about 'Central Park', crawling with exiles from all over the world,

> A civilisation without a soul, in search of one?

---

[1] Has no ruined castles, no marble buildings.

There is a parallel quick tour through the culture of Europe, at any
rate those elements of it that meant most to Auden. But we do not
encounter any real poetic feeling until he comes to terms

> Of images that I have seen,
> And England tells me what we mean . . .
> Always my boy of wish returns
> To those peat-stained deserted burns
> That feed the Wear and Tyne and Tees . . .
> An English area comes to mind,
> I see the nature of my kind
> As a locality I love,
> Those limestone moors that stretch from Brough
> To Hexham and the Roman Wall,
> There is my symbol of us all.

It is only in such places, such flashes, that one gets a glimpse of the
heart – which is what makes for poetry; all the rest is mind, and his
indomitable will to write verse, whether poetry or not.
  The conclusion of it all is modest enough:

> O every day in sleep and labour
> Our life and death are with our neighbour,
> And love illuminates again
> The city and the lion's den,
> The world's great rage, the travel of young men.

In May 1941 the Auden–Britten operetta, *Paul Bunyan*, was given
half-a-dozen performances at Columbia University. Auden was
everywhere well, and generously, received by the academic world,
though there were some difficulties when Chester accompanied him.
Paul Bunyan was a folk hero of the early American lumbermen. So
we may see this work as an attempt on Auden's part to graft himself
into the American past. We may compare it with Eliot's determined
attempt to sink shafts, in every way, into the historic English past –
notably with 'East Coker', from which place the Eliots had
emigrated to Puritan New England in the 1630s. In the church there

was already a window to them, and now too are his ashes. He sent me a proof of the poem, and was pleased at my emphasising its historical significance in my review of it. A further demonstration of Wystan's intention to identify himself with America was his application for citizenship.

For the year 1941–2 he was teaching at the University of Michigan, where he confessed he felt very lonely and low. This was just as I felt later out on the prairie at Urbana, where the State legislature of Illinois had, in the goodness of its heart, placed its original 'cow-college' as far as possible from the temptations of wicked Chicago. Myself, I was disappointed – still lonely at the University of Wisconsin at Madison, though less so, for I had two libraries there in which to research for my book *The Cornish in America*.

This was not a happy year for Wystan. In August his mother died – a worse shock than he had expected – and he wrote that he had been going through 'a great personal crisis'. He was always reticent about his personal feelings – a deep defect of his poetry: poetry exists to express them. Altogether this was a complex matter: uprooting himself, adapting himself to a new environment; complications with Chester and Britten, who did not like each other; Britten's increasing wish to free himself from Wystan's influence, the concentrated impact of his personality, and the determination to develop his own with the help of the genial Pears.

For three years, 1942–5, Auden taught at high-minded Quaker Swarthmore, helped out by teaching the girls at neighbouring Bryn Mawr. (There I had a friend, but forgot my engagement to lecture). These teaching engagements over years, and frequent lectures here, there and everywhere, helped to build up a large academic audience for his poetry – and further increased the didactic tone of his work, distancing himself from it when it should have been more personal and intimate. It was as if one couldn't penetrate the reserve – in contrast with Eliot, with whom one always feels in personal touch for all his reserve.

The two works of these years were brought together in one volume, under the title of the second, *For the Time Being*, in 1944. Eliot gave it a laudatory puff. 'Mr Auden's virtuosity has perhaps been overemphasised by his critics: it has not been cultivated for its

own sake, and must be viewed in relation to a profounder evolution.'
I doubt that. 'His skill in versification and his personal idiom are no
less vigorous in *For the Time Being* than in any previous book.'
Agreed. 'But they distract the attention less, and interpose less
obstruction between the reader and the meaning than ever before.
The meaning is not easy, and perhaps not easily acceptable; but we
think that this is the best book (leaving his dramatic work out of
account) the author has produced since *The Orators*.'

I do not agree: I agree with the majority verdict that the two
intervening volumes of poetry are best. Eliot went on to some special
pleading to recommend the two works, arguing that 'they are
related; though the relationship may be apparent only after they
have been given the close attention they deserve.' It is not apparent to
me, nor to anybody else: both works are obscure.

The first work, *The Sea and the Mirror*, is described as 'A
Commentary on Shakespeare's *The Tempest*'. Does the Preface give
us a clue?

> Well, who in his own backyard
> Has not opened his heart to the smiling
> Secret he cannot quote?

(Why not? That is what poetry is for – to express it.)

> Which goes to show that the Bard
> Was sober when he wrote
> That this world of fact we love
> Is unsubstantial stuff . . .

I have sometimes wondered if Wystan was sober when he wrote
much of this work.

The subject, we apprehend, is what happens *after* the play – an
interesting and original idea. The characters explain themselves –
their characters are discernible – if only they would explain themselves and what they are thinking more clearly. Prospero has a long,
obscure farewell to Ariel. The characters are on shipboard:

> Dotted about the deck they doze or play.

They are on their way homeward, to what fate or purpose is as obscure to them as to us. Antonio is depicted as a loner, and has a refrain as such. Gonzalo has a speech which offers some clarity:

> Evening, grave, immense, and clear,
> Overlooks our ship whose wake
> Lingers undistorted on
> Sea and silence: I look back
> For the last time as the sun
> Sets behind that island where
> All our loves were altered . . .

For this relief we are grateful; as also for

> Farewell, dear island of our wreck.
> All have been restored to health,
> All have seen the Commonwealth,
> There is nothing to forgive.

But in fact there *was*: Prospero's extrusion from his dukedom by his brother and his setting adrift on the open sea with his daughter. The subject of Shakespeare's play is the retribution for this, and Prospero's eventual return. Alonso's speech to his son offers some advice:

> Expect no help from others . . .
> The Way of Justice is a tightrope
> Where no prince is safe for one instant
> Unless he trust his embarrassment.

We note Auden's addiction to superfluous subjunctives. The Master and Boatswain are in character:

> At Dirty Dick's and Sloppy Joe's
>   We drank our liquor straight,
> Some went upstairs with Margery,
>   And some, alas, with Kate;

> And two by two like cat and mouse
> The homeless played at keeping house.

Here is an Auden touch; and here another, if adopted from Housman:

> And hearts that we broke long ago
> Have long been breaking others.

Other recognisable touches are the obsession with sex:

> Pure scholarship in Where and When,
> How Often and With Whom...

and

> Every gorgeous number may
> Be laid by anyone.

Sebastian is 'wicked still'; Miranda has an intelligible speech, a nice poem. But nothing happens, nothing at all; the longest item is a long-drawn-out speech by Caliban, which is unintelligible: a parody of Henry James. But what is its purport?

> If now, having dismissed your hired impersonators with verdicts tanging [ranging?] from the laudatory orchid to the disgusted and disgusting egg, you ask and, of course, notwith-standing the conscious fact of his irrevocable absence, you instinctively *do* ask for our so good, so great, so dead author to stand before the finally lowered curtain and take his shyly responsible bow for this, his latest, ripest production, it is I – my reluctance is, I can assure you, co-equal with your dismay....

This is comparatively intelligible, but one *is* dismayed by the nearly forty pages of rather distinguished, if long-winded, prose that follow, and added up to – well, what? We are conceded occasional simple sentences, like 'there is probably no one whose real name is

Brown'; or 'I introduced statistical methods into the Liberal Arts. I revived the country dances and installed stoves in the mountain cottages. I saved democracy by buying steel. I gave the caesura its freedom.' I think the Muse is supposed to be speaking, but am not sure.

What does it all add up to?

Mandarin literature at that time prided itself on obscurity. Paul Valéry's longest poem, *La Jeune Parque*, is mostly unintelligible, except for a few lines which Maurice Bowra, as a classical scholar, extracted from the beginning. I think it was the cult of Words as such that misled them, as with Auden. When the painter Degas brought to Mallarmé the poems he had written, the poet instructed him that poems were not written from ideas, *'mais avec les mots'*. When I am confronted by Auden's obscurity I remember the Victorian joke about Browning's 'Sordello', of which only the first and last lines were intelligible:

> Who will shall hear Sordello's story told . . .

and after several hundred lines,

> Who would has heard Sordello's story told.

But this is no longer a Mandarin world: let us above all be clear.

I find the second piece, *For the Time Being*, equally opaque. It is described as 'A Christmas Oratorio', and is dedicated to Wystan's mother, Constance Rosalie Auden, 1870–1941, with an epigraph from St Paul: 'What shall we say then? Shall we continue in sin, that grace may abound? God forbid.' St Paul, we know, was neurotic; all the same, I found it a little odd that committed Christians, like Wystan and his tutor Nevill Coghill, did not allow that to inhibit their sexual pleasures. One would have thought . . . but perhaps that was rather puritanical of me.

The formal structure of the piece is recognisable, if little else is. It is that of the Christian myth: Advent, the Annunciation, the Temptation of St Joseph, the Summons, the Vision of the Shepherds, At the Manger, the Meditation of Simeon, the Massacre of the Innocents, the Flight into Egypt.

There are a Narrator, Recitative, Chorus, Semi-Chorus, the whole lot. Again they are given intelligible sentences, recognisable disparate thoughts, if we do not much agree with them:

The two sexes at present are the weak and the strong;

such portentous phrases as 'the fern's devotion to spatial necessity'; 'the plants are indignant'. (Are they?)

Only now it's no longer real; the real one is nowhere
Where time never moves and nothing can ever happen.

We recognise not only the common cliché of the thirties, the 'real', whatever that bee in their bonnet buzzed to them, but the influence of Eliot that is constant throughout, in the pretentious statements meaning not so very much:

For the garden is the only place there is, but you
                          will not find it
Until you have looked for it everywhere and
                   found nowhere that is not a desert.

Untrue.

And life is the destiny you are bound to refuse until
                   you have consented to die.

I regard this denial of life as immoral; I always disapproved of it in Eliot's work – just because his own personal life was miserable. When he at long last found happiness with his second marriage the doctrine disappeared; so did the inspiration. Misery, nerves on edge, gave him inspiration (as physical pain and mental anguish did me).

The Inevitable is what will seem to happen to you
                   purely by chance;
The Real will strike you as really absurd.

A lot of the disparate thoughts are, in my opinion, just words:

> And who knows if it is by design or pure inadvertence
> That the Present destroys its inherited self-importance?

Philosophy, according to the Wise Men, observes

> That Truth is knowing that we know we lie.

The Shepherds reply,

> On strange beds then O welcome home
> Our horror of home.

Eliot had made horror fashionable: 'O the horror!' (More appropriate today would be, 'O the squalor!')

> The Exceptional is always usual
> And the Usual exceptional –

pure Eliot. Oh, stuff it, Uncle Tom, one is inclined to say, and to recall Henry Reed's exact parody:

> *vento dei venti*,
> The wind within a wind unable to speak for wind.

'Simeon's Meditation' strikes me as nothing but verbiage: 'Before the Positive could manifest Itself specifically, it was necessary that nothing should be left that negation could remove.' He is accompanied by the Chorus enunciating such profound thoughts as

> We have right to believe that we really exist.

I would not pass these strictures if they did not lead to a critical point – a lot of Auden's thinking extrapolated simply from a word; even a rhyme just gave him the thought that followed. This is not necessarily an objection; it is one of the uses of rhyme that it makes suggestions and suggests ideas. (Contemporary uncooked poetry misses that help.) The point is that, often with Wystan, the thought itself, which should be seeking expression and take precedence, is missing.

In the section, 'The Annunciation', the Four Faculties describe themselves. 'Thought' itself has for company

> an embarrassed sum
> Stuck on the stutter of a decimal –

a striking phrase, but what does it mean? And there

> To Be was an archaic nuisance.

For Feeling we read

> Of hunchbacks hunting a hermaphrodite,

while Sensation (is Sensation a different faculty from Feeling?) is represented by this:

> In a wet vacancy among the ash cans
> A waiter coupled with a crow.

In such passages we know where we are: it is the disease that runs through all modern literature, of being original at any cost, at the cost of any sense, persuasiveness, conviction.

In 'The Temptation of St Joseph' something of the crisis Wystan went through in his relations with Chester is discernible, if only through a glass darkly. Wystan had come through a very serious temptation: his love was so intense – he thought that he had discovered a permanent 'marriage of true minds' – that he could have murdered Chester's lover, as he confessed. 'There are days when there will never be a place which I can call *home*, that there will never be a person with whom I shall be one flesh, seems more than I can bear.' When he had come through the crisis he wrote, 'poets are tough and can go through the most dreadful experiences.' (So I have found: solipsism is a great, if impoverishing, refuge.)

He said, 'Joseph is me'. Something of the experience is to be overheard in 'Caught in the jealous trap/ Of an empty house I hear/ As I sit alone in the dark/ The drip of the bathroom tap/ The creak of the sofa spring/ . . . Father, what have I done?' (One has to learn the hard way, from a similar experience, not to be jealous.)

Only one section persuades me and is convincing, the long prose speech of Herod in 'The Massacre of the Innocents'. This is ironical, and Auden had a distinct gift for parody. I am charmed by Herod's remark, 'O dear, why couldn't this wretched infant be born somewhere else? Why can't people be sensible?' He is reluctantly obliged to order the Massacre of the Innocents (for which there is no historical warrant, by the way). My marginal comment at the time reads, 'excellent *advocatus diaboli*'. That at the end of the book sums up: 'One is not moved for a single moment by anything in either piece. Two failures.' I see no reason to revise that opinion.

At the end of the war in 1945 Auden was given a job by the American Army to go to Germany and report on the psychological effects of bombing on civilians. He was granted temporary status as Major and turned up in England on the way, his first visit since 1939. His old friends were affronted at the line he took: not the least embarrassment, but complained of the cold in English houses, the food, and that London hadn't suffered much. In fact the country was utterly exhausted after six years, food rations low, the people undernourished, fuel scarce, nerves on edge. His friends found his behaviour insufferable, and hard to explain. Was it bravado, braving things out? I think not: there was a real strain of insensitiveness in him, of not noticing other people's reactions or perhaps not caring much what they thought.

He came down to All Souls, a rather comic figure, ungainly in his ill-fitting army uniform, holding forth loudly, his voice very noticeable with the American accent he had adopted – the short a's: he 'laffed' for he 'laughed'. Not unnatural to me, for short a's are regular in West Country and North Country speech. In his case they were brought out aggressively, and were as ill-fitting as his uniform. I didn't have much talk with him, merely exchanged a few jokes about 'spectacled sailors', a phenomenon of the US Navy, unfamiliar in the RN.

He had found his job in Germany interesting, the spectacle shattering. He had been billeted in the house of a believing Nazi, who at their defeat poisoned wife and grandchildren, and then himself. He should have begun and ended with himself: I have no sympathy for deliberate idiots. It was like the Mitford sisters' friend, Dr Goebbels, poisoning all five or six kids, then wife and himself. I recalled the Nazi commandant at St Malo, who, after Germany's surrender, blew up the historic old city out of spite. Auden was upset by the effects of the mass-bombing and surprised by the systematic organisation of the extermination of the Jews, though he recognised that 'the obtuse Krauts' could be cruel. What he did not realise was that Professor Lindeman, the German-American scientist whom we both knew at Christ Church, Churchill's adviser, was convinced that only hammering over the head would teach them. This it seems to have done.

On his return to New York Auden's citizenship papers came through – an American citizen at last. In London he had expressed his preference for life over there to his old friends – 'a large, open impersonal country'; I think that that genuinely answered to something in his own nature. Note the accent on the *impersonal*. 'The attractiveness of America to a writer,' he said, 'is its openness and lack of tradition. It's the only country where you feel there's no ruling class. There's just a lot of people.'

Isn't this rather superficial, taking the surface of things for the reality? Auden was no historian and no politician: the truth about such a vast amorphous society covering a whole continent is much more complex. There *is* a ruling class – the middle-class (to which Wystan belonged; *ich nicht*). It is true that it is an open society, but it does not lack tradition. There are in fact two: that of New England, and that of the South, both of them strong and distinguished (in both senses). Out of the union of these two the United States was forged in the American Revolution.

Openness has its disadvantages, as well as its advantages – especially for American writers, those who have difficulty in finding their roots and are for ever digging them up and exposing them to the light of day – not good for the roots or their work. This is not true of those who have roots – either in New England, as so many had in the nineteenth century, or in the South, in the twentieth century. But many feel rootless. Others preferred an aristocratic tradition, richer, more varied, diversified and coloured – like Henry James and Edith Wharton, Santayana, Eliot and Pound. Isn't there a certain colourlessness in Auden's work? Besides rootlessness? His culture is wide rather than deep, discursive, ranging over the surface rather than sinking shafts into rich ground.

Eliot came to England to sink shafts into a deeper tradition. He was fortunate to become eventually a cultural mentor, a kind of twentieth-century Dr Johnson in London, which he could not bear to leave. As for Wystan, Eliot's wife described him later to me as an 'Ishmael, wandering over the face of the earth'. There is grave danger for an artist in pulling up his roots, as so many *émigrés*, particularly Russian, have found.

Auden's next book, *The Age of Anxiety*, 1947, was awarded a Pulitzer Prize. Henceforth prizes, assignments, lectures, engagements mounted up. He gave Connolly, who was chronically hard up, money as another reason for preferring the United States – he would never have been so well off in Britain. He would be able now to spend summers in Ischia and later buy a property in Austria, then back to Oxford and, when he died, was thinking of returning to New York.

This way of life, with all the attendant publicity, was not good for poetry. When Paul Valéry became an international literary figure, he complained bitterly to Gide of the waste of time and energy – no more poetry. Robert Frost – who had had his London period when young – was a better model in holding to his surly solitude: the poetry remained with him to the end.

What light does *The Age of Anxiety* throw on the writer we are sleuthing in his work? Well, he had great luck with his title: it caught on, it was representative of the appalling age we had been living through, and were to continue to do. Eliot, as its publisher, gave it as usual his careful backing. 'The content of the poem will arouse endless discussion and argument; the form is one more illustration of the author's inexhaustible resourcefulness and mastery of versification, which becomes more astonishing with every work that he puts forth.' True enough, but note that Eliot does not say anything about the content. What is it about? It is hard to say.

Dedicated to Wystan's old Oxford friend, John Betjeman (a dearer friend to me), it is described as 'A Baroque Eclogue'; I do not know how the word 'baroque' applies, and it is certainly not an eclogue. The versification is a remarkable *tour de force*: written in varied measures, but with a ground-bass of the medieval consonantal metre of *Piers Plowman*. Here was something that he owed to the Eng. Lit. School at Oxford, for his tutor, Nevill Coghill, was a leading authority on Langland.

The work is not a bit like Betjeman's (which I much prefer), though dear John certainly suffered from *Angst* all right – in that sense the dedication is appropriate. The piece is more of a masque, with characters speaking (one of them Quant, named from *The Turn of the Screw*, a masterpiece of *Angst*). A brief masque is incorporated; from a long Prologue we pass to 'The Seven Ages', 'The Seven Stages', 'The Dirge', 'The Masque', to 'The Epilogue'. With some prose mixed with the verse, it is rather like a return to *The Dance of Death*.

The Prologue is dominated by the theme of war:

> Untalkative and tense, we took off
> Anxious into air; instruments glowed,
> Dials in darkness, for dawn was not yet;
> Pulses pounded; we approached our target,
> Conscious in common of our closed Here
> And of Them out There thinking of Us. . . .

This affords us not only a specimen of the virtuoso versification but of the regular trick of personifying abstracts, turning other parts of speech, adjectives, adverbs, prepositions into nouns, which we can address.

As always I like the descriptive passages best, and he does succeed remarkably in turning this ancient Middle English measure into poetry at times:

> Our long convoy
> Turned away northward as tireless gulls
> Wove over water webs of brightness
> And sad sound. The insensible ocean,
> Miles without mind, moaned all around our
> Limited laughter, and below our songs
> Were deaf deeps, denes of unaffection . . .

With that word 'unaffection' perhaps we approach the man we are pursuing. As more obviously in, 'Yes, America was the best place on earth to come to if you had to earn your living – but did it have to be so big and empty and noisy and messy?'

Here and there we can recognise the reticent poet revealing himself – one of

> The creative odd ones the average need
> To suggest new goals.

Perhaps I might interpose here to explain that in this Langland measure not only consonants clang (Eliot's word to me about what he wanted in 'East Coker') but also initial vowels do, any vowels count, as above 'odd ones', 'average'.

Any further clues? There is the idiosyncratic attitude to sex. In peacetime people can be 'happily certain that the one with whom they shared their bed last night will be sharing it with them again the next, and who, in consequence, must be written off by the proprietor as a lost market.' 'In times of war even the crudest kind of positive affection between persons seems extraordinarily beautiful, a noble symbol of the peace and forgiveness of which the whole world stands so desperately in need.'[1] Whether a noble symbol or not, it was true that in wartime everybody looked for consolation. Then again, we find the old complex in 'the grace of person which grants them [youth], without effort on their part, a succession of sexual triumphs. For then the longing for success, the doubt of ever being able to achieve the kinds of success which have to be earned. . . .' We recognise the signature tune. We note too the uprooted:

[1] cf. my poem, 'An Episode in the Korean War', in *A Life: Collected Poems.*

Many about much, but remain alone,
Alive but alone, belonging – where? –
Unattached as tumbleweed. Time flies.

Tumbleweed is American, we do not have it in Britain.

We have an important clue in this: 'Human beings are, necessarily, actors who cannot become something before they have first pretended to be it. And they can be divided, not into the hypocritical and the sincere, but into the sane who know they are acting and the mad who do not.' We have seen that he was, from undergraduate days, always acting a part. (Was he also acting a part as an American? – those aggressive short a's!) I totally disagree with the sentiment: it is clean contrary to my own gospel. I believe that it is fundamental for people to find their own true self, their deepest and truest self, not always easy, and thus to fulfil their own best nature. And not to be too self-conscious about it, in Wystan's public school manner. The dedicatee of the book, John Betjeman, had a public school self-consciousness and people always thought that he was playing a part – as he was; but the part he played was himself: from his schooldays he was entirely original, not like anybody else. He did not need to put on an act: he was that act, endearing eccentricities and all, they were part of him.

What I do agree with is the direct indictment of Man: 'the torpor of his spirit, the indigent dryness of his soul, his bottomless credulity, his perverse preference for the meretricious or the insipid.' I place the 'bottomless credulity' at the top of the list: the credulity that could lead a whole nation to vote for a Hitler and then be surprised that it led them into war; to vote for appeasing Hitler, and then to be no less surprised that it led them into war. It is *not* any original sin that is the trouble, in accordance with C.S. Lewis's nonsense, but simple human stupidity – and Wystan's phrase 'torpor of spirit' is applicable to it.

Again I am not impressed by his improbable appositions: 'the mountains are amused' (are they?); 'geometers vexed by irrelevant reds'. They are there to make a startling effect. They do not impress a simple proletarian like myself, though they may the middle-class girls of Bryn Mawr – and America is fundamentally a middle-class society. (Eliot and Henry James opted for aristocratic standards; so do I.) Still less can I agree with the conclusion with which the book ends: the return to 'the actual world where time is real and in which, therefore, poetry can take no interest.'

That is an inversion of sense, just bad thinking. Practically the whole of Thomas Hardy's poetry is immersed in the sense of time; Shakespeare's Sonnets are full of the sense of the passing of time.

In 1949 Auden was invited to give the Page–Barbour Lectures at the University of Virginia, which form the book *The Enchafèd Flood*, subtitled 'The Romantic Iconography of the Sea'. He begins by doffing his cap to Professor Wilson Knight, who had written a book, *The Shakespearean Tempest*. This professor, with his Second Class in the Eng. Lit. School at Oxford, was quite unable to see the obvious person depicted in the Sonnets, with all his obvious characteristics and circumstances: Shakespeare's one and only acknowledged patron, young Southampton. We do not have to attach much importance to the myth-thinking of such a person, who, for the rest, saw homosexuality in all the subjects he wrote about in his books, without value.

This prose work of Auden's is another example of Eng. Lit. myth-thinking. 'Sky as contrasted with water = Spirit as contrasted with Nature. What comes from the sky is a spiritual or supernatural visitation. What lies hidden in the water is the unknown powers of nature. ... The degree of visibility = the degree of conscious knowledge.' What is the value of that sort of information, if that is the word for it? In *Moby Dick* Ahab's losing a leg is a 'castration symbol'. To the factual-minded historian losing a leg is just losing a leg.

And the historian prefers to get facts right. Auden lays down that 'the characteristic of the Romantic period is that the artist, the maker himself, becomes the epic hero, the daring thinker, whose deeds he has to record. Between about 1770 and 1914 the great heroic figures are not men of action but individual geniuses, both artists and, of course, scientists.' What are the facts? Who were the heroes of and to the nineteenth century? In Britain, Nelson above all; Raglan, of 'The Charge of the Light Brigade', not Tennyson who wrote about it; gallant little Bobs, Lord Roberts of the March to Kandahar; Captain

Scott of the Antarctic. In the United States, Robert E. Lee, Stonewall Jackson, Abraham Lincoln. All men of action.

No doubt it is donnish of me to correct Wystan and point out what the facts are; I dare say that this partly accounts for the wary attitude of his group towards me, ensconced at Oxford, entrenched in All Souls. I fear I must correct him even on a point of ethics. 'The ethical hero,' he says, 'is the one who at any given moment happens to know more than the others.' No, dear: not *knows*, but *acts* better – a criminal might actually *know* more.

Auden had a curious *penchant* for wasting time on the nonsense of theology – in this like Eliot. He was a friend of Reinhold Niebuhr, a good man who was a friend of all good causes, generous and charitable, but rather a platitudinarian. He and his wife were very kind to Wystan when he first arrived in the US, and he used to discuss theology with the high-minded couple, as well as the state of the world. Here Auden lays down, 'There cannot be a kingdom of heaven whose values are completely other than the kingdom of this world.' I do not know what 'the kingdom of heaven' means, and from my reading it does not appear that anybody else does either. In such a case we should take the advice of the philosophic Wittgenstein and say nothing of that of which nothing is to be said.

This is not to disparage Auden's discursive reading, the range of which is quite remarkable. It is no less fashionable, or was: there they all are – Kierkegaard, Nietzsche, Baudelaire, Rimbaud; and, for an American audience, Whitehead (another expatriate), Herman Melville, and Marianne Moore whose profound remark about the sea is quoted: 'It is human nature to stand in the middle of a thing; but you cannot stand in the middle of this.'

An historian does not much respect myth-thinking; myself, I prefer a modest, factual Eng. Lit. book on this theme, Anne Treneer's *The Sea in English Literature*.

Auden's next volume of poems, *Nones*, 1951, is named after one of the canonical Hours into which the Church divided the set hours of prayer during the day. Eliot, in publishing it, gave Wystan the usual boost: 'an intellectual poet whose technical resourcefulness is always equal to the ceaseless development of his mind and sensibility; a poet who never arrests his progress or repeats himself.'

This is over-generous; 'technical resourcefulness', certainly; but I do not think that there was much development in Auden's mind, there was a certain static quality about it, and he did repeat himself. Eliot was himself anxious not to do that. When I suggested that after his play about Thomas Becket, he might give us one about Thomas More, he replied that he couldn't write another play about a Thomas. He wished each work of his to be different, to tackle something new, and that he couldn't write poetry unless he thought of it as a problem to be solved.

This is surely very odd: a crossword-puzzle mind – and indeed he solved *The Times* crossword puzzle every morning to keep himself in training. Wystan also was a regular addict of crosswords, and one can watch his addiction to rare words needing a dictionary in this volume. Can one imagine a poet like Hardy spending time on crosswords? He relied more on the heart for inspiration, and moves one more.

The volume is dedicated to the religious Niebuhrs, lines that express disillusionment with contemporary demotic society, newspapers concocting

> . . . spells to befuddle the crowd,
> All words like peace and love,
> All sane affirmative speech,
> Had been soiled, profaned, debased
> To a horrid mechanical screech . . .

Now,

> . . . little was left standing
> But the suburb of dissent.

That certainly speaks for me. This links up with a tribute to earlier society, in 'The Managers':

> In the bad old days it was not so bad:
> The top of the ladder
> Was an amusing place to sit; success
> Meant quite a lot – leisure

And huge meals, more palaces filled with more
    Objects, books, girls, horses
Than one could ever get round to, and to be
    Carried uphill while seeing
Others walk.

Pride of place is given to a favourite poem of his, and a favourite with others, 'In Praise of Limestone'. In it we can see him:

If it form the one landscape that we the inconstant ones
    Are consistently homesick for, this is chiefly
Because it dissolves in water. Mark these rounded slopes
    With their surface fragrance of thyme and beneath
A secret system of caves and conduits; hear these springs
    That spurt out everywhere with a chuckle
Each filling a private pool for its fish and carving
    Its own little ravine, whose cliffs entertain
The butterfly and the lizard;examine this region
    Of short distances and definite places.

This is the region of the North Country, the 'Paradise' he told me he could never return to: a contrast with the immense distances and indefinite places of America. At a party which Perry Knowlton gave for me, down in Greenwich Village, Wystan spoke to me of it. He came over, having heard 'a Limey accent'. Really! This was putting on an American act for my benefit: an Oxford accent was familiar and normal enough speech to him.

He went on to speak of Cornwall, for which he had a certain feeling, a phrase now and again in the early poems. The Cornwall he liked was that which I don't much care for, the derelict mining area of the West, the ruined engine-houses with their tall stacks, the slag-heaps and waste. He wanted to tell me about the geology – a genuine interest of his – and the books in which to read it up. I knew the books, and was not interested.

A passage in the poem, also, I did not like:

What could be more like Mother or a fitter background
    For her son, for the nude young male who lounges

Against a rock displaying his dildo, never doubting
    That for all his faults he is loved, whose works are but
Extensions of his power to charm?

There we have Wystan, exposing himself. I objected to the phrase, in
my marginal note; not that I was, I hope, conventional and 'square',
but that it stuck out unnecessarily in the poem, disproportionately
drawing attention to itself, a piece of bravado. Later, he changed it to
read,

                    . . . the flirtatious male who lounges
    Against a rock in the sunlight.

Some critics have objected to his revisions; I do not object to their
toning down the rhetorical and challenging bravado. I do not care
for the continual exaggerations – 'the graves flew open, the rivers ran
up-hill'; or 'the crime of life is not time'. And here is an example of
word-thinking: 'limbs became hymns' – in no sense could they. The
thought did not come first, and then the word to express it; the word
came first, but does not even suggest a thought. This is what is meant
by verbiage, of which he was an addict, like smoking or Benzedrine.
    With that goes the cult of rare words. Eliot was addicted to the
dictionary for the meanings and definitions of words, their different
senses; Auden just picked them up and stuck them in like shells or the
glittering pieces of quartz he admired. In leafing through the volume I
note merely a few: cerebrotonic, dedolant; megalopods, gennels,
mornes, mammelons; sossing, sootering, baltering, faffling, sotter-
ing; frescade, hideola, jussive, prosopon, catadoup. One ought not
to need a dictionary to read poetry in one's own language.
    However, the technical mastery is undoubted, the sheer variety of
measures. And in some poems one observes – what the ordinary
reader might not – the internal rhymes (I favour and use them myself,
nobody notices):

Somewhere are places where we have really been, dear spaces
    Of our deeds and faces . . .
Dogs bark in the dark . . .
                the special case of their place.

Of places, some poems recall Ischia where he resided in the spring and summer most of these years, 1948–57. A longish poem describing life there is dedicated to Brian Howard, an exact contemporary of Harold Acton and mine at Christ Church, therefore Wystan's senior by a few years. He had a gift for writing, but early extinguished his promise in drink and drugs. (I knew him only by sight when we were undergraduates, mad, bad, and dangerous to know.)

> I am presently moved
> By sun-drenched Parthenopeai, my thanks are for you,
> Ischia, to whom a fair wind has
> Brought me rejoicing with dear friends
>
> From soiled productive cities. How well you correct
> Our injured eyes, how gently you train us to see
> Things and men in perspective
> Underneath your uniform light.

That is something that an old-world civilisation can do for one after all; and behind that pleasant, sybaritic life,

> Dearest to each his birthplace; but to recall a green
> Valley where mushrooms fatten in the summer nights
> And silvered willows copy
> The circumflexions of the stream . . .

beside this my note reads, 'We could wish this more often' – evidently instead of the abstractions, the rhetoric, banging the drum. I like a quieter poetry.

He was capable of that, as in several poems here:

> As I listened from a beach-chair in the shade
> To all the noises that my garden made –

evidently Ischia, not New York.

We are back in the city with 'In Schrafft's', a popular restaurant on Fifth Avenue, which used to be both reasonable and good. There he watched the clients and wrote them down (as I have done). Here was one who

> When she lifted her eyes it was plain
> That our globular furore,
> Our international rout
> Of sin and apparatus
> And dying men galore,
> Was not being bothered about.

We are back in the modern world,

> And the truth cannot be hid;
> Somebody chose their pain,
> What needn't have happened did.

Auden could command direct plain speech when he chose:

> I could (which you cannot)
> Find reasons fast enough
> To face the sky and roar
> In anger and despair
> At what is going on,
> Demanding that it name
> Whoever is to blame.

The historian knows well enough, as the philosopher Santayana knew, who was to blame, who loosened the avalanche in 1914. It has never ceased its malign movement since.

We track down Wystan to his holiday shack on naughty Fire Island outside New York,

> ... this outpost where nothing is wicked
> But to be sorry or sick ...

where

> The Love that rules the sun and stars
> Permits what He forbids.

We note the curious contradiction, without any tension between the two, which I have mentioned; and

> Look outward, eyes, and love
> Those eyes you cannot be.

There is Wystan.

Brian Howard put his finger on what is to me an important defect, the lack of visual sense in the poetry – not complete, but there is little of it, and I prefer the descriptive passages where it is present. This obviously has some relation to his extreme short-sightedness – and that again may enter into his intense concentration on the word on the page. It may also have a literary source, in the too contemptuous reaction against Georgian poetry, finding its subject in countryside, field and meadow, birds, nature – the poetic revolution heralded by two Americans, Pound and Eliot. Eliot hardly notices a flower, except the blue of larkspur because it is Our Lady's colour.

In this year, 1951, Auden had a most interesting job, writing the libretto for Stravinsky's opera, *The Rake's Progress*, based on Hogarth. Here was another expatriate, uprooted from his own culture, an exile from the terror of the Russian Revolution, far worse than anything Auden had encountered in the thirties. I consider that uprootedness is the trouble at the base of Stravinsky's later music, and regard only the earlier – up to, say, the *Sinfonie des Psaulmes* – as really inspired.

I have never seen or heard *The Rake's Progress*, but the collaboration was a success: it holds the stage still. Stravinsky was immensely impressed by Auden's facility and speed in writing the text, though reluctant to admit Kallman into the billing. Here was a field in which Wystan was indebted to Chester, the more musical of the two, with a special knowledge of opera. Henceforth they collaborated on a number of such jobs: an *Elegy for Young Lovers*, performed at Stuttgart; *The Bassarids*, at Salzburg; *Love's Labour's Lost*, in Brussels. *The Rake's Progress* had a grand première in Venice. One sees what a cosmopolitan figure Auden became.

I don't want to go into the awkward subject of his relations with Chester, though they were the central feature of his life and had their influence in his work. I used to hear from a Jewish woman friend, of the *New York Times* circle, that Chester became rather uppish about his writing and treated Wystan *de haut en bas*. One has known that happen, when a *protégé* one has coaxed along to fulfil himself, in the end takes a high line with one.

Wystan had educated Chester. I have always regarded his taking on the responsibility for this wayward youth as a tribute to his Christian character, recognising a moral obligation in spite of many *contretemps*. Fairly early on Chester, not in love with Wystan, declared himself in love with someone else. At once physical relations ceased. This is exceptional in its absoluteness, and must represent something important. It shows that Wystan really loved Chester, who on his side had affection for the man of genius who provided for him and looked after him to the best of his ability – no easy task. Of course he could well afford it now, and eventually left Chester everything, who survived him by only six months. That much has to be said.

This gradually came to be only intermittent companionship, leaving Wystan desperately lonely – and that became a chief motive for his finally leaving New York for Oxford. When he came back from six months in Europe, he did not continue his affair with his woman friend (he assured her that bed was lonely without her), who went on to marry someone else. What a mix-up it all was! (I could not have borne it for a moment – so squalid.) So unlike the chaste bachelor housekeeping of Eliot and John Hayward.

In these years he continued to have remunerative academic assignments, with the girls at Mount Holyoke and then at Smith College – which has a splendid collection of French Impressionists. I have never forgotten them – I don't suppose that they made any impression on Wystan. However, there is no doubt that he was a gifted and conscientious teacher, who gave good value for money. Money poured in – he was careful about it, and saw to it that he got his share of the returns on *The Rake's Progress*. He was now writing far more prose, frequent articles and reviews in any number of

papers, interviews, people asking for his opinion on this and that –
which he was always only too ready to give. He complained himself,
'It is a sad fact about our culture that a poet can earn much more
money writing or talking about his art than he can by practising it.'

With all these activities the impulse towards poetry was swamped,
and henceforth prose – plenty of it – was in the ascendant. *The Shield
of Achilles* showed deterioration: logomachy taking the place of
inspiration.

Then, again, luck came his way: he was elected Professor of Poetry
at Oxford for five years. This was a prestigious post, which had been
held notably by Matthew Arnold, though the prestige went down
when C.S. Lewis had managed to fork in a mild, unpoetic cleric, one
Adam Fox, against E.K. Chambers and my candidate, David Cecil.
Auden restored the prestige of the Chair. It was only a part-time
affair; he could get his lectures into one term each year, but it gave
him a pulpit, and enabled him to spend more time in Europe, with a
convenient base at our old college, Christ Church.

4

Between America and Europe

Auden enjoyed his spell as Professor of Poetry at Oxford, though he complained of the inadequate remuneration. It was on account of that that he was specially allowed to concentrate his three annual lectures into one term, reasonably enough – or else, as he said, he would have been out of pocket in travelling to give them. He had other complaints to make of the impoverished country, ruined by the war. In the United States he wouldn't open his mouth for less than $300, often a poetry reading – he was not a good reader of poetry, as Eliot was – brought in $1,000. Here he was offered £5 for a lecture.

The fact was that he was spoiled by the Americans. His rather inferior volume of verse, *The Shield of Achilles*, got the National Book Award; the Poetry Society of America awarded him their Gold Medal; the complacent Academy of Arts and Letters welcomed him to their body. He had become used to adoration; I don't think it turned his head, but in the vast US there is so much more room on the ground that they can afford to be, and are, more generous.

Still, he knew what the score was. When the posturing poetaster, Allen Ginsberg, tried to kiss the hem of his trousers in the cathedral at Christ Church, it didn't prevent him from calling his poetry rubbish – but privately; he was tactful about that sort of thing, careful not to create enemies.

And he gave more than his money's worth as Professor. His lectures were crowded – this was quite unusual: his fame was a draw. I have attended one of H.W. Garrod's lectures as Professor, when the audience was hardly a dozen. I didn't attend any of Wystan's, for I was by now mostly in the United States myself. I was back for one Encaenia when he made his (too long) Latin oration, written for him by the Public Orator – an anachronistic performance, which he carried off with his usual nonchalance and erratic pronunciation.

He was never embarrassed. One weekend he was staying in Edinburgh with our All Souls friend, Archie Campbell, to preach in St Giles's (shades of Jenny Geddes!), and Wystan's dentures broke on the Sunday. The Professor of Dentistry did an emergency job – and Wystan preached his sermon.

At Oxford he gave occasional parties in his rooms in the Christ Church Annexe. Better, he had regular sessions in the Cadena Café, where undergraduates could meet him and submit their work or discuss anything. He was a born teacher, with his clerical and clinical background. At Christ Church he regularly attended early service in the cathedral.

The young William Walton had been a choirboy and received his early musical education there. Then Wystan and he were neighbours at Ischia. They collaborated in a work for our old college, 'The Twelve'. I did go over to the cathedral to hear it, but failed to respond either to the words or the music. Again, it is only Walton's early work that I like – truly inspired, the later not. However, Simon Preston, the organist, good musician that he is, liked it; so I suppose I am wrong. For liturgical music I prefer early polyphonic music, Tallis, Palestrina, Byrd – or that splendid Christ Church composer, Taverner.

In this later period prose came to dominate – no crime – but it was a pity that there was so much of it in Auden's verse. *The Dyer's Hand* contains the Oxford Lectures, and more: a fat book that could do with slimming, in the way Eliot slimmed his. At the same time one must pay tribute to the intellectual vitality, the remarkable range of reading; it is full of insight and reflection. Also, it is more personally revealing than the poetry, as if in that he was acting up to a persona: this is more informal, Wystan in undress.

The book is dedicated to Coghill, 'a tutor in whom one could confide' – there were no secrets between those two. At the outset he says something surprising: 'There is something, in my opinion, lifeless, even false, about systematic criticism.' Even I do not go so far as that, though I think there is immeasurably too much of it today, strangling rather than encouraging creativeness. Still, there is a place for it, provided critics know its place, which is a secondary one, an aid to the understanding and interpretation of creative art, not an end in itself.

I agree with him about that. He asks, what is the function of a critic? He then lists half-a-dozen functions, all of them practical and subordinate. Such as – introducing one to authors and works one hadn't heard of; correcting one's undervaluation (or overvaluation?) of author or work; showing relations between works of different ages and cultures; throwing light upon the processes of artistic creation and the relation of art to the life and society out of which it comes. Note that he says nothing about criticism as judgment, though I see a place for that, a reasoned estimate of works of art, applying comparative standards, giving reasons, and with justice of mind – rarest of qualities. In fact the vast bulk of criticism, or what passes for such in reviews, is largely a matter of personal preference, emotional thinking, preconception or prejudice.

He says sensibly, 'The critical opinions of a writer should always be taken with a large grain of salt' – I suppose because his own involvement gets in the way, and it is difficult for him to distance himself enough to be objective. He adheres to the traditional view that the purpose of reading is to give pleasure: 'Pleasure is by no means an infallible critical guide, but it is the least fallible.' We should add that there are other purposes, information for one, or where should we be? Since we are looking for him in his work we might ask how much of it gives pleasure. I must honestly say, not much – chiefly the shorter poems, not much of the longer.

He provides us with some of the information about himself, of the kind he would like to have when reading other critics.

Eden. Landscape: Limestone uplands like the Pennines. A precipitous and indented sea-coast. Climate: British. [This is surprising.] Ethnic origin of inhabitants: Highly varied as in the United States [this was tactful], but with a slight Nordic predominance. Language: Of mixed origins like English, but highly inflected. Weights and Measures: Irregular and complicated. No decimal system. Religion: Roman Catholic in an easygoing Mediterranean sort of way. Lots of local saints. Public Entertainments: Religious processions, brass bands, opera, classical ballet. No movies, radio, or television. Sources of Public Information: Gossip. Technical and learned periodicals, but no newspapers.

This does add up to a self-portrait of a sort, though it is not complete or wholly reliable. Naturally he says nothing about his tastes in regard to sex; I always knew that he was a great gossip, but in fact he was addicted to newspapers, especially the Sunday papers with their book pages, which he would rush out to get.

A section of the book is valuable for the light it throws upon America, American society and culture – a far more complex subject than Europeans realise. (It took me years to get the hang of it.) He approaches this via Henry James's critical attitude towards the American scene.

The features which most struck the analyst then are those which most strike the immigrant now, whether they be minor details like the magnificent boots [Wystan always wore carpet slippers, for his flat feet and corns] and teeth, the heavy consumption of candy, 'the vagueness of separation between apartments, between one room and another, between the one you are in and the one you are not in'; or major matters like the promiscuous gregariousness, the lack, even among the rich, of constituted privacy, the absence of forms for vice no less than for virtue, the 'spoiling' of women and their responsibility for the whole of culture, above all the elimination from the scene of the squire and the parson.

To this he adds, truly, enough, the excesses of climate – but then America is a continent.

He then goes in for some philosophic reflection. 'What in fact is missing, what has been consciously rejected, is the *romanitas* upon which Europe was founded and which she has not ceased attempting to preserve.' I think I glimpse what he means, though he goes on to some vague theorising about virtue as opposed to liberty. He sees a contrast between an ordered, hierarchical, authoritative society as against a disorderly, horizontal, democratic one. (In the circumstances it is the chief political miracle of the age that such a vast continental society achieves order at all, and on the basis of liberty: no Siberia.)

He concludes that the cost of liberty as the dominant principle is 'extremely high, and to some may seem prohibitive' – as it did to Henry James and Eliot. It is not for me to suggest that a price that has to be paid for so much liberty is a high degree of social conformity, at least on the surface; but that is characteristic of a middle-class society. One may well prefer the eccentricities, the humours and ironies, of an aristocracy.

In considering the poetry of Robert Frost, Auden notes that there are American characteristics not to be found there, 'the absence of which implies disapproval: the belief, for instance, that it should be possible, once the right gimmick has been found, to build the New Jerusalem on earth in half-an-hour'. In other words, the optimistic American Dream – it has had some shattering blows since he wrote. 'One might describe Frost as a Tory, provided that one remembers that all American political parties are Whigs.' One can put it more simply: Frost did not subscribe to the Liberal illusions so dear to middle-class Americans. He was not the poet of modern America; but a countryman of an older world, New England, who could sum up the story in a line:

The land was ours before we were the land's.

Auden says that 'the commonest human situation in his poetry is of one man, or a man and wife, alone in a small isolated house in a snowbound forest after dark'. I was reproved by Edmund Wilson for writing of 'the loneliness that is America'. He said that he had never found it lonely. But he had always lived in communities, Princeton and Harvard, on crowded Cape Cod or in the bars of New York. He had never tried living out on the prairies. Anyway, the crusty old liberal ended up utterly disillusioned with the Dream, and described himself as 'an internal exile'. (As I am, from demotic society.)

Auden's mind was discursive, slipping quickly here and there all over the place, instead of the slow, plodding mind of the historian, patiently and systematically investigating. It has taken the Elizabethan historian twenty years to solve the problems of Shakespeare's biography, and of his autobiography in the Sonnets. Nor could this ever have been done so long as the line prevailed that one did *not* want to know anything about the life of the writer or the experience that went into his work. As a better scholar than Auden, Professor John Holloway, says: 'What begins for the student of literature as background was for the author intense with the very quality of life.'

Auden was a genius, though not a scholar – so the don does not hold his Third in the Schools against him, though he does the Second Classes in Eng. Lit. of such Shakespearean 'experts' as Wilson Knight and Kenneth Muir. As academics they should have done better, and taken note of the essential point made by a First Class mind like John Holloway's. We absolutely *need* to know about the historical background, the life and experience, that went into Shakespeare's work – as much as Herman Melville's, or Poe's, or Wilde's, whose biographies Auden deals with.

'On principle,' he says, 'I object to biographies of artists, since I do not believe the knowledge of their private lives sheds any significant light upon their works.' This is simply silly, contrary to common sense – a position he took up when young and then stuck to without thinking into and out of it. And it involved him in contradictions, apologising for having to go into the biography when dealing with Wilde, or the acutely personal with Cavafy. 'Reading any poem of his, I feel, "This reveals a person with a unique perspective on the world."'

The same holds good for Shakespeare, only one needs all the more the aid one can gather, for his work comes to us out of the sixteenth century, four hundred years ago, while Cavafy's belongs to the twentieth, with which we are so much more familiar, for it is our own. Auden's approach to Shakespeare is thus in terms of the twentieth century, with its fashions and prejudices and hobbies. We know what Auden's were, so we are not surprised when he tells us, *tout court*, that Antonio in *The Merchant of Venice* is homosexual.

There is not the slightest evidence that Shakespeare thought in such terms – it does not occur in the life of that heterosexual, a family man, again infatuated with the young dark lady; it occurs in all we know about Christopher Marlowe and all through his work. So much for the intimate – and obvious – relation between the person and his work.

Of *The Winter's Tale* he lays down that 'Leontes is a classical case of paranoid sexual jealousy due to repressed homosexual feelings.' This is the kind of view fashionable in Auden's intellectual circle, and in accordance with his own bias. There is no evidence that this is Shakespeare's view of the case; and ordinary common experience tells one that a straight heterosexual is much more likely to be jealous of a friend's dealings with his wife than a homosexual would be.

So it is not surprising that he got the facts about William Shakespeare mostly wrong, since he says several times over that we 'know nothing about him', that he is 'fortunately anonymous'. An Elizabethan scholar knows that we know more about William Shakespeare than about any other Elizabethan dramatist – except for the later life of Ben Jonson. Auden repeats the old hoary nonsense about the Sonnets: 'We know almost nothing about the historical circumstances under which Shakespeare wrote these sonnets' – Wystan should have asked the leading historian of the time, who could have told him. 'We don't know to whom they are addressed or exactly when they were written.' We do: they were addressed to the obvious person, Shakespeare's young patron, and they were written during the obvious years, 1592–4, when he was writing *Venus and Adonis* and *The Rape of Lucrece* for him and dedicating these publicly to him. The Sonnets were private.

I give Wystan credit for seeing the obvious point that so many others have missed, that 'Mr W.H. is not the friend who inspired most of the sonnets but the person who secured the manuscript for the publisher.' That is correct: actually he was Southampton's stepfather, Sir William Harvey; but people who are not Elizabethan scholars do not know that it was the usual thing – and the regular rule in the House of Commons – to refer to a knight as 'Mr'.

I don't blame Wystan for not knowing that piece of historical information – few do; but he should have asked. At the time of the

Quatercentenary, 1964, I had produced the answers to all these questions, except for the identity of the Dark Lady. That came later, as a bonus – I should never have discovered her if all the previous answers had not been completely correct (they are all now definitive and unanswerable, the problems properly solved).

At that time the BBC asked Auden to hold forth – they did not ask the authority who had solved the problems. I remember being angry at Wystan then getting Southampton wrong, proclaiming him as a heterosexual![1] Actually he was bisexual. The Sonnets begin with an attempt to persuade him to marriage, which he rejected, not as yet responsive to women. Later, Shakespeare was worried that the young man's first experience with women should be with the promiscuous Emilia, through the poet's fault, introducing them.

All this was beyond the comprehension of Victorian, and Victorian-minded, professors. My dear old friend, Quiller Couch, would have been shocked if he had known the facts. But he specifically disclaimed wanting to know. This is what is meant by obscurantism – and it is a curious phenomenon, incomprehensible to an historian: rejecting knowledge! Quiller Couch got his Second in Greats at Oxford, simply through neglecting the History side of the School. His colleague in editing the Cambridge Shakespeare, Dover Wilson, got a Second in the Historical Tripos – and got the Sonnets completely wrong, never even saw that Mr W.H. was the publisher's man, not Shakespeare's. But nobody had done. These people should take note of the findings of First Class minds. I know well that this is a donnish thing to say – but what are dons *for*, but to say them?

In 1960 Auden produced a volume of shorter poems, *Homage to Clio*, a provoking title for, as we have seen, he had not an historian's sense of history – too discursive and undiscriminating. We might pause at this turning point to consider a fellow poet's assessment of his work to date – that of Philip Larkin, who kept his inspiration, like Housman, almost to the end, they wrote so little and didn't spread themselves or sprawl.

---

[1] In reprinting this piece Auden omitted the howler.

In reviewing *Homage to Clio*, 'What's Become of Wystan?'[1] Larkin said severely that the past twenty years – i.e. the American period – had added little to justify his reputation. The book (Eliot did not give it a boost) 'marks the end of the third decade of Auden's poetic life and does not alter the fact that almost all we value is still confined to its first ten years'. What had gone wrong? 'He has remained energetic and productive; his later work shows the same readiness to experiment with new and (in theory) maturer themes; he has not lost his sense of humour. And yet no one is going to justify his place in literary history by *The Shield of Achilles*' – which had been given the National Book Award in the US, with not much critical sense.

Larkin went on to sum up to date.

He was, of course, the first 'modern' poet in that he could employ modern properties unselfconsciously ... modern also in an effort to put poetry at the service of the working-class movement.

Larkin regarded him as completely confined to his time:

Few poets since Pope have been so committed to their period ... we find the Depression, strikes, the Hunger Marchers; we shall find Spain and China; above all we shall find not only the age's properties but its obsessions: feeling inferior to the working class, a sense that things needed a new impetus from somewhere, seeing out of the corner of an eye the rise of Fascism, the persecution of the Jews, the gathering dread of the next war. It is precisely this dominant and ubiquitous unease that lay at the centre of Auden's verse and which he was so apt to express.

He was certainly the voice of That Time, the appalling thirties, and, as we have seen, spoke for me.

Larkin, who belonged to a generation younger than ours, that of the 'next war', goes on:

[1] *The Spectator*, 15 July 1960.

I have stressed this identification to make clear why Auden's outlook was completely dislocated when it [That Time] ceased. This came about in two ways – by the outbreak of war in 1939, and by Auden's departure for America a few months earlier. At once he lost his key subject and emotion – Europe and the fear of war – and abandoned his audience together with their common dialect and concerns. For a different sort of poet this might have been less important. For Auden it seems to have been irreparable.

Larkin means that it would have been less important for a poet who was not so *engagé* and had not set so much store by it, made it a main theme. We have seen how decisively Auden and Isherwood disengaged themselves on the boat going over. It is always a dangerous thing for a writer to pluck up his roots (I was aware of that in half-going to America later). And I have made the point that Auden was the loser by missing the grandest, most noble and tragic experience of the century, the heroic years 1940–5, when Britain held out to save Europe and civilisation.

There is a further point. In conversation with Robert Lowell in New York once, he said to me that there was something in the American atmosphere that was inclement for English poets, blighting to the spirit. (What is it? The materialism of American life, from which Eliot fled?) Certainly Louis MacNeice felt it and came back – to become a better poet, in the long run, than Auden. Britten felt it, and returned to fulfil his genius beyond all hope and expectation. He had specifically feared cutting himself off from his *roots*.

There is no doubt that Auden's poetry lost its inspiration and fell off. What was he to do? From indications in what he said about Tennyson and others, the problem became, what was he to do to fill in? Tennyson filled in by writing a lot of unsuccessful plays; Browning by a mass of prosy stuff in the form of verse; Swinburne by repeating himself without inspiration; Bridges with dead academic verse dramas; Morris with tedious renderings of the sagas. And so on. I have said that professional poets usually write too much: they go on and on. Auden did well to take to prose, less well to become a public figure. America encouraged that, and Larkin considered that he ended up a pompous 'wind-bag'. I think that unfair.

Larkin's assessment of the American period continues uncompromisingly.

His first three American books were long, ambitious, and stylistically variegated, yet held the reader's attention only sporadically if at all. The rambling intellectual stew of *New Year Letter* was hardly more than a vamp-till-ready; *The Sea and the Mirror* was an unsuccessful piece of literary inbreeding; while although in *For the Time Being* Auden works hard to reinvigorate the Christian myth as a poetic subject, he is too often chilly ('weave in us the freedom of/ The actually deficient on/ The justly actual') or silly ('It was visiting day at the vinegar works'). As for *The Age of Anxiety*, I never finished it, and have never met anyone who has.

Well, I have, though I admit it was a struggle: it does not stand up to Auden's test of giving pleasure. Larkin appreciated the danger of rootlessness, and thought at that juncture that 'if his poetry could once take root again in the life surrounding him a new Auden might result, a *New Yorker* Walt Whitman viewing the American scene through lenses coated with European irony.' (Americans are without irony.) This was not to be. Wystan did not even respond with poems about American landscapes, as I did, appreciatively, but also to console myself for loneliness. Eliot sank roots again in the landscapes of East Coker, Burnt Norton and Little Gidding – and produced poetry out of them. And out of religion. Auden returned to regular religious observance, but no religious poetry came out of it, as with John Betjeman. So far from 'rooting' himself in America, he upped sticks again and made for Europe – Ischia, Oxford, then Austria, Oxford, to die in Vienna. It was sad.

Larkin was rather supercilious as a man, and patronising in his criticism; extremely careful of his own public image, as he let out to me, registering as usual. A misanthrope ought not to care about what people think of him. We can be kinder, and more just, to *Homage to Clio* and find some good things in it, the simpler and more personal the better. 'The More Loving One' is a good poem:

> If equal affection cannot be,
> Let the more loving one be me.

There is Wystan in his sad relationship with Chester; we recognise it again in a passing phrase,

> to throw away
> The tiniest fault of someone we love . . .

He put up with a great deal from that quarter, without much return after all; I regard it as very Christian of him. With his blatant ways Chester involved himself in some trouble in Ischia – as Charles Osborne says, it was time for them to move on. (Wiser not to live one's private life in public, in the full glare of the sun.) 'Goodbye to the Mezzogiorno' is Wystan's farewell piece, with its typical 'throw-away' concluding lines:

> To bless this region, its vendages, and those
>   Who call it home: though one cannot always
> Remember exactly why one has been happy,
>   There is no forgetting that one was.

One reason for that is clear, though he was not one of those

> believing *amore*
> Is better down South and much cheaper
> (Which is doubtful) . . .

I could not appreciate a move away from Italy to any German country: Wystan – very wary with me – explained it in linguistic terms, he preferred the German language to Italian. This seems odd to me, though understandably he did not want to live in Germany. Searching for a home, he found it in a pleasant little village in Austria, Kirchstetten, in the countryside outside Vienna. Here he is buried, far from his beloved limestone country. What a Hejira! Was he flying from himself? Was all that repeated rejection of the personal a desire to protect some inner vulnerability?

The main feature of the book is a long prose Interlude, 'Dichtung und Wahrheit' (Poetry and Truth, after Goethe): 'An Unwritten Poem'. It begins, 'Expecting your arrival tomorrow, I find myself thinking *I love you*: then comes the thought – *I should like to write a poem which would express exactly what I mean when I think these words.*' Very well then, why not write it? Or try to?

Instead of that we are given a dozen pages of gnomic utterances, oracular statements, garrulous discussion around and about the subject in general. My marginal comment when I read this unsatisfactory substitute for a poem, if ever he intended to write it, was 'Perverseness – allowing cleverness to get in the way'. Another comment was, 'Like Eliot, *creating* difficulties instead of making things simple'.

I do not propose to follow them, simply pinpoint what reveals Wystan. The poem he would like to write is not concerned with fictitious characters, 'but with my proposition *I love You*, where *I* and *You* are persons whose existence and histories could be verified by a private detective'. After a lot of patter we come to, 'The I-feeling: a feeling of being-responsible-for'. My comment was, 'Considerate and solicitous!' After more argy-bargy we come to his having read 'far too many love poems written in the first person'. My marginal note says, 'Certainly there are far too many conventional hetero love poems'. But that means that the unwritten poem could have been something different and much more original.

Wystan tells us, 'I cannot know exactly what I mean'. We might take this candid outburst to apply to many more obscure passages in his work. He never would explain them – 'your guess is as good as mine,' he would say – perhaps he couldn't. And I am not impressed by literary 'explication', explaining *obscurum per obscurius*. 'Words cannot verify themselves.' Can't they? 'So this poem will remain unwritten.'

A pity: a long poem on the complex subject of his relations with Chester would have been remarkable. After all, Benjamin Constant achieved something of the kind, in prose, in *Adolphe, Romans* and *Meredith*, in verse, in 'Modern Love'.

The piece ends in Wystan's comic mood, with a throw-away line: 'What have I promised? *I will love you whatever happens, even though you put on twenty pounds or become afflicted with a moustache.*' Funnily enough, this is more or less what came about. It looks as if Wystan went on loving, in adverse circumstances, by an act of will as he went on writing verse.

This is contrary to my idea of writing poetry – only when the heart moves or is moved. No one could say that his long piece about the queer domesticity of Kirchstetten, 'On Installing an American Kitchen in Lower Austria', was poetry. This was for another of Chester's talents which he took no trouble to hide, his cooking:

> Though built last May in Austria
> Do-it-yourself America
> Prophetically blue-printed this
> Palace kitchen for kingdoms
> Where royalty would be incognito, [etc.]

Nor do I propose to follow Wystan in his tricks and inversions of sense, which run like a disease throughout modern literature. (Like Sartre's idiotic pronouncement that Soviet Russia is the incarnation of human freedom.)

> The watch upon my wrist
> Would soon forget that I exist,
> If I were not reminded
> By days when I forget to wind it.

The comment here reads – Wystan had an attentive reader in his old friend – 'The fact is the converse: historians state facts'. He was very strongly against corrupting the language, which everything in demotic society is out to do – all the media, advertising of every kind on every available public space, especially in America, where one is worn down by the perpetual solicitation of eye and ear, filling every vacuity, fearful of leaving oneself with one's thoughts for a moment.

> To their credit, a reader will only perceive
> That the language they loved was coming to grief,
> Expiring in preposterous mechanical tricks,
> Epanaleptics, rhopalics, anacyclic acrostics.

Comment here: 'Sheer cleverness does not produce poetry, only verse.'
I am more amused by Wystan's light verse about our friends:

> T.S. Eliot is quite at a loss
> When clubmen bustle across
> At literary teas,
> Crying: 'What, if you please,
> Did you mean by *The Mill on the Floss*?'

And, *pace* Larkin, there are simply charming simple lines – which show that Wystan could do it if he chose – to our acquaintance at the House, Canon Claude Jenkins, on his eightieth birthday. There are the well known features of Christ Church:

> The tribes who study and the sporting clan
> Applaud the scholar and approve the man,
> While, in cold *Mercury*, complacent fish
> From well-fed tummies belch a birthday wish.

I did not 'applaud the scholar' or 'approve the man': of wide and scatter-brained learning, he never wrote a thing, so it all died with him; and he was a horribly dirty old fellow, tobacco, snuff, wine stains all down his front, I couldn't bring myself to speak with him.

In 1964 Auden received an official invitation from the government of Iceland to revisit the island – receptions, parties, dinners, staying with the British ambassador, etc. He had become an international figure. Was this worth the rootlessness that went with it? No; contrary to creativeness, which needs silence and solitude. He was coming to terms with the drying up of inspiration:

> Bullroarers cannot keep up the annual rain,
> The water-table of a once-green champaign
> Sinks, will keep on sinking: but why complain? Against odds,
> Methods of dry farming may still produce grain.

This was very reasonable: he turned more to writing verses for special occasions, birthdays, festivals, obituaries, and for particular people, especially in his vast international circle of friends. Actually, I like many of these later, simpler poems more than the more pretentious formal pieces.

He also wrote a good deal of pornographic verse – after all, one must amuse oneself, and one's friends. John Betjeman, though an almost sanctified cult figure, wrote a lot of this stuff in earlier years; even the venerated Eliot wrote some naughty unpublished poems. (I have written very few – and, as usual, kept them to myself.) I do not propose to go into this aspect of Wystan's talent, but merely quote the first stanza of a very long, unpublished piece, since it depicts him in a familiar stance:

> It was a Spring day, a day for a lay, when the air
> Smelled like a locker-room, a day to blow or get blown;
> Returning from lunch I turned my corner and there
> On a nearby stoop I saw him standing alone.

There is Wystan, and no doubt about the talent.

Iceland was followed by six months in Berlin, as writer-in-residence, paid for by the Ford Foundation. I suppose this was part of the re-education of Germans to take their part in civilisation, to which they had done so much damage. (When I was asked to go at the time of the Berlin Air-Lift, and even pressed by Bevin himself, I refused: I had had more than enough of them. As Coleridge had found, there was a Nimiety, a too-muchness about the Germans.)

Contrary-wise Auden was anti-French: 'Their famous *clarté* is thicker than the thickest *Wiener* treacle.' This was pure prejudice, one of those positions he had earlier taken up and regularly stuck to. Actually, French *clarté* is exactly what he and his group, especially Spender, most stood in need of.

On this return to Kirchstetten Wystan wrote what his biographer regards as 'the third of his key love poems'. It is not really a love poem, but something more original, as was the relationship. Hugerl was a Viennese call-boy, who regularly came out to console Wystan during periods at Kirchstetten when he was left there on his own, with Chester more and more in Athens. So the poem balances delicately between affection and finance, mutual understanding, and a certain loyalty, as may obtain in such circumstances.

> Hugerl, for a decade now
> My bed-visitor,
> An unexpected blessing
> In a later life
> For how much and how often
> You have made me glad . . .
>
> How is it now between us?
> Love? Love is far too
> Tattered a word . . .
> Glad that I know we enjoy
> Mutual pleasure:
> Women may cog their lovers
> With a feigned passion,
> But males are so constructed
> We cannot deceive.

He always took the position that no one could object to mutual if momentary pleasure. A hardly less satisfactory relationship was that with the housekeeper, who looked after the place and cooked; but she went and died:

> *Liebe Frau Emma,*
> *na, was hast Du denn gemacht?*
> You always made
> such conscience of our comfort,
> oh, how could you go and die,
>
> as if you didn't know
> that in a permissive age
> so rife with envy,
> a housekeeper is harder
> to replace than a lover.

True enough.

No one, however, replaced Chester, though he ceased to accompany Wystan to New York now for the winter, leaving him lonelier there than ever. In Austria they coincided for the summer, and there they worked together on libretti for operas. The love of opera Wystan had got from Chester, who had now become a seasoned librettist himself. One sees the domesticity at Kirchstetten from a poem for Chester:

> Martini-time: time to draw the curtains and
> choose a composer we should like to hear from,
> before coming to table for one of your
> savoury messes.

(Mightn't that have been written out as well in prose?)

In 1961 they had written together a libretto, *Elegy for Young Lovers*, for whom a young German, Henze, composed the music: it was performed at Stuttgart. In 1966 all three co-operated again in a bigger affair, *The Bassarids*, performed at Salzburg. These were the manic followers of Dionysus according to the *Bacchae* of Euripides, of which Professor E.R. Dodds at Christ Church – friend of Wystan and Louis MacNeice – had edited a good text. At some point the couple made their own libretto for a Mozart opera, but this did not achieve performance. Their final effort in this genre was a version of *Love's Labour's Lost*, which was produced in Brussels. The music was composed by the too diversely talented Nabokov. I am no authority on opera, and cannot speak of any of these works; still, I cannot believe that Nabokov's music would be much good.

Even performances in Vienna were not what they had been – in the 1920s one heard Strauss conduct his own operas there. Now –

> Standards at the Staatsoper
> steadily decline each year,
> and Wien's become provincial
> compared to the Pride she was.
> Still it's a cosy country,
> unracked by riots and strikes,
> and backward at drug-taking.

Wystan himself habitually took Benzedrine in the morning, to pep him up for work; and a sleeping pill at night to send him off at once. More and more pickled in drink, he took to having a bottle of vodka at his bedside by night.

I do not know what effect these artificial aids had on his health; but from his sixties his face presented an extraordinary corrugated map of wrinkles – an off-putting lizard-like integument. Perhaps fifty cigarettes a day (ugh!) had something to do with it. He took it all as a matter of course, never thought to desist from his disgusting habits. He would joke about his countenance being like 'a wedding cake left out in the rain.' David Cecil said, 'Were a fly to try to cross it, it would break its leg.'

The summer of 1968 saw the overthrow of a comparatively liberal Communist régime in Czecho-Slovakia by force from Moscow. Auden reacted with all his old liberalism:

> The Ogre does what ogres can,
> Deeds quite impossible for Man.
> But one prize is beyond his reach,
> The Ogre cannot master speech.
> About a subjugated plain,
> Among its desperate and slain,
> The Ogre stalks with hand on hips,
> While drivel gushes from his lips.

The drivel was of course Communist orthodoxy: he had come a long way from the naïve Communist sympathies of the thirties.

In fact he supported the original American involvement in Vietnam, as I did. One must not forget that the motive was the right and proper one of rolling back Communist expansion – and if the United States had not put up a struggle that expansion would have got much further. No one can think that the extension of Communist rule in that area has brought anything but unrelieved suffering to the people there.

He now had no use for fellow-travellers in Britain like Kingsley Martin, for so long and so deleteriously editor of the *New Statesman*, which misled a whole generation of young people week by week. Kingsley Martin was not a bad man, and he was not a Communist; he was merely inside-out: whatever his own country did was wrong, whatever its enemies did was right. He – along with the disastrous Dawson of *The Times* – was the only editor to advocate the dismemberment of Czecho-Slovakia for the benefit of Hitler. And Kingsley Martin a man of the Left! Auden wrote, 'I'd gladly string him up with my own hands'. More mildly, I would merely have had him horse-whipped. But he would probably have liked that, for he was a raging masochist.

That year Auden gave the first T.S. Eliot Lectures founded at Canterbury. Very appropriately – and we must notice that his prime interests now were opera libretti, and writing prose. Much of his verse now was, like most of contemporary 'poetry', prose cut up in lines to look like verse. The Lectures were published with the title *Secondary Worlds*: the terms Primary and Secondary World he had got from Tolkien, a very odd figure in the Eng. Lit. landscape at Oxford. I suppose he had genius – he was difficult enough to warrant it. Wystan was an addict of his writings and of the world of imagination he created; one must remember that he had been brought up on Icelandic Sagas, the subject of the second Lecture.

The third was on 'The World of Opera'. He tells us, revealingly of himself, 'From the verse-play to the opera libretto is a short step'. In opera the words are secondary to the music; one might almost say that they are tertiary, less important than the acting, gestures and mime. He himself says that one can go along for considerable passages without understanding the words. However that may be, it excuses us from undertaking a study of his and Mr Kallman's (as he always referred to him publicly) libretti.

He gave *The Importance of Being Earnest* as an example of verbal opera, where the characters have no importance apart from what they say; the sole purpose of the plot is to give opportunity for their remarks. He concluded that 'opera is the last refuge of the High style', and, laying down the law as usual, that there could be no more epic or grand tragedy.

Let that be as it may, a dominant concern of his last period was the corruption of language, which he regarded, rightly enough, as 'enormously encouraged by mass-education and the mass media'.

One sees how sensibly conservative his thinking had become: almost a Johnsonian figure – except that that rôle was more effectively exercised by Eliot remaining in London.

He concluded with his view that 'poetry is personal speech in its purest form'. Very well: then why reject the personal from consideration of the work?

Next year appeared *City Without Walls*, dedicated to another of his innumerable friends, Peter Heyworth:

> At Twenty we find our friends for ourselves,
> but it takes Heaven
> To find us one when we are Fifty-Seven.

(Does it? It depends what one is and looks like.) The title poem presents an appalling picture of contemporary society:

> Hermits, perforce, are all today.

When he says 'all', he means all of us, the few, the elect. (I was lucky to have withdrawn long before, when I saw what was coming, from 1945, the 'Welfare State' and all that, onwards.)

> What they view may be vulgar rubbish,
> What they listen to witless noise . . .

In the context one should italicise the word *they*.

> For what to Nothing shall nobodies answer?

> Quite soon computers may expel from the world
> all but the top intelligent few.
> Today we smile at weddings
> where bride and bridegroom
> were both born since the Shadow
> lifted, or rather
> moved elsewhere: never as yet
> has Earth been without
> her bad patch, some unplace with
> jobs for torturers . . .

(Why not print as prose, for is it poetry?)

He now finds more satisfaction in remembering the happier past. An agreeable subject is his Eulogy of his old tutor Coghill at Exeter College. Let us print it as prose. 'Blessed be Christ Church/ for having been so snooty forty years ago/ about Eng. Lit./ What reason/ had I to suppose/ Exeter worth a visit?' Coghill is praised for being 'not a disciple-hunting, Socratic bully'. This describes C.S. Lewis: he found no disciple in John Betjeman, who hated his Socratic logic-chopping, and got his own back with

> Objectively, our Common Room
> Is like a small Athenian state –
> Except for Lewis: he's all right
> But do you think he's *quite* first rate?

We see Auden himself as an undergraduate: 'a time to wear odd clothing/behave with panache/and talk nonsense as I did/ambling in Oxford's/potamic meadows with friends.'

We see him thirty years before 'motoring towards mountains/ joyfully certain nightfall/would occasion joy./It did. In a flagged kitchen/we were served broiled trout/and a rank cheese; for a while/ we talked by the fire/then, carrying candles, climbed/steep stairs. Love was made/then and there: so halcyoned/soon we fell asleep/to the sound of a river/swabbling through a gorge.' But for the alliteration and one word 'swabbling' it might be prose.

He included a Prose Prologue for the *Son et Lumière* programme at Christ Church in the summer of 1968. A 'Prologue at Sixty' went back to boyhood and

> added to its names my numinous map
> of the Solihull gas-works, gazed at in awe
> by a bronchial boy, the Blue John mine,
> the Festiniog railway, the Rhayader dams,
> Cross Fell, Keld and Cauldron Snout . . .
> or modern holies, Middagh Street,
> Carnegie Hall and the Con-Ed stacks
> on First Avenue. Who am I now?

An American? No, a New Yorker,
who opens his *Times* at the obit page.

Observe the alliteration all through: it helps to make it poetic. There are the places of youth's 'Paradise' he could never go back to. Middagh Street is where he lived when he first came to New York. (When in the city I always stayed next to Carnegie Hall for the music – and what music one heard!)

Among the marginalia occurs: 'Few can remember/clearly when innocence came/to a sudden end,/the moment at which we ask/for the first time: *Am I loved?*' There was the obsession, from the beginning to the end.

'Doggerel by a Senior Citizen', of 1969, looks back over the perspective from which he had come, and sums up usefully for us the final position at which he arrived.

> My family ghosts I fought and routed –
> Their values though I never doubted:
> I thought their Protestant Work-Ethic
> Both practical and sympathetic.

All we need question here is the first line. What was wrong with his family that he should have contested? He was fortunate to have been born into it – lettered and cultivated, solicitous and loving, proud of their precocious boy. We note that their values were middle-class, believing in work and a responsible attitude towards society.

We should remark here a difference from Isherwood, which those unacquainted with the subtleties of the class structure in Britain are unaware of. Isherwood was not middle-class, but upper-class; his family were gentry, from whom and whose values he really revolted. He was a rebel, Wystan was not: one notes the lack of social responsibility in the odd *égaré* course Isherwood followed, ending up in the right place for such, among the pacifists, Hindu mystics and other humbugs in Los Angeles. Apart from his sex life – about which Wystan was rather more circumspect than Isherwood, who made a career out of his – Auden was rather a conformist.

When couples played or sang duets
It was immoral to have debts:
I shall continue till I die
To pay in cash for what I buy.

Very middle-class of him, and very unlike the hire-purchase, consumptionist society inspired by the ideas of his old patron Keynes. And we remember that it was his mother who first introduced him to *Tristan and Isolde*, the boy Wystan taking the woman's part.

The *Book of Common Prayer* we knew
Was that of 1662:
Though with it sermons may be well
Liturgical reforms are hell.

Here again I agree with him; brought up like him rather old-fashioned High Church (*not* a Cornish Nonconformist, and therefore never a Liberal), I cannot find my way round in the new liturgy. Wystan ceased going to the Episcopal Church he had attended in New York, and took to the Greek Orthodox Mass, with its vastly ancient tradition, and at Kirchstetten regularly to the Catholic parish church. At Oxford there was always Christ Church cathedral.

Nor are those Ph.Ds my kin
Who dig the symbol and the myth:
I count myself a man of letters
Who writes, or hopes to, for his betters.

In that he was like all cultivated people, few as they are – as against the vast mass of half-baked academics with their cult of the Ph.D, weighed down by theory, and explication, and 'evaluation'. Nice to know that Wystan had no use for it – and those of us in the game know how ludicrous it is that numbers of the least intelligence all want to write a thesis on T.S. Eliot.

Among the many odd jobs that Auden industriously picked up in New York, regularly adhering to his work-ethic – 6.30 or 7 a.m. till well into the afternoon – was that of translating the private 'Jottings', a kind of spiritual diary kept by Hammarskjöld, the Secretary-General of the United Nations. Auden much admired this remarkable Nordic figure with the enormously lofty brow, a repressed homo. Like Thomas Mann, Hammarskjöld regarded himself as, if not the Deity, at least his deputy in this wicked world. He was at the top of his *réclame* in co-ordinating all the world to resist the Anglo-French attempt to stop Nasser in his tracks over Suez in 1956. This was a pitiably easy job – and a great pity that Nasser was allowed to get away with it, de-stabilising the Middle East ever since.

Knowing no Swedish, Auden co-operated with a translator in putting the moral perfection of this work into perfect prose – it became a great best-seller, after the author's death on a futile trip to lay down the law between warring tribes in Africa. In his summing-up of this archangel Auden dared to raise a doubt about the privileged intimacy of his intercourse with the Deity. The Swedes tried to get him to correct this minimal qualification; Auden conscientiously refused, saying, 'There goes the Nobel Prize.'

And so it transpired or seems to have done; at least he did not get it. He told me at Oxford that he was the runner-up, I do not know to whom.

Winters in New York had become cheerless without Chester, and Wystan was saddened by Stravinsky's death there. At last he was becoming doubtful about his health, after all the strain he had put upon it – he had always had exceptional vitality and nervous strength, but what a *train-de-vie* he had subjected them to! He was pickled in drink and smoke. He had a feeling that a heart attack might get him, with no one in call for days. Sometimes there was a call – a threatening one.

At length he decided, 'New York is hell', and made preparations to return to Oxford.

5

Return to Europe: Oxford, Austria

Through all his tergiversations, his adventures in mind and body, Auden had wisely kept his relations with his old college at Oxford in good repair. At a Christ Church Gaudy in 1960 he proposed a toast in verse:

> Ah! those Twenties before I was twenty . . .
> In Peck [Peckwater Quad] there were marvellous parties
>   With bubbly and brandy and grouse,
> And the aesthetes fought with the Hearties
>   It was fun, then, to beat the House . . .
> One could meet any day in Society
>   Harold Acton, Tom Driberg, or Rowse:
> May there always to lend their variety
>   Be some rather odd fish at the House.

Needless to say, I was not a member of Society, and never attended any of those marvellous parties in Peck. I lived in Meadow Buildings on the next staircase to Harold Acton, whom I knew through contributing poems to *Oxford Poetry*, the *Oxford Outlook*, and, I suppose, was better known as a fanatical young Labour man. That odd fish, Tom Driberg, I hardly knew; and Wystan, in gentlemanly fashion, asked permission to use my name.

Never a Prodigal Son, he was welcomed back by Christ Church, which hospitably placed at his disposal a little cottage, a converted brewhouse, on the way into the Meadows from St Aldate's. Just across the street is Old Mother Sheep's shop of *Alice in Wonderland*. He should have been happy there – but again he was lonely.

While the cottage was being got ready for him he came to stay with us in All Souls for a month. The very first morning after breakfast he came to tell me that he had been burgled in the night. I said to him, 'But didn't you sport your oak?' He had left his outer door unlocked. We resumed relations on the old footing of years before, with me as his senior giving him a lecture on how things had changed. When we were young we never dreamed of locking our doors, such was our blissful security. Now, in filthy modern society, there was no security, everything had to be locked up. I had had two fine rugs stolen while away from my rooms, in America; undergraduates would steal each other's wireless sets; Oxford was a prime burglar area, etc. In addition there were confidence tricksters – and Wystan had been tricked by one of these.

A young fellow had come to his rooms with a sob-stuff story about wife-and-child and no money (without money he shouldn't have embarked on wife and child) – would Auden lend him £50? Out of Christian charity Wystan made out a cheque for him. Meanwhile, this representative of the new social order took his bearings. That night – Wystan as usual going to bed early at 9 p.m. – the contents of his wallet, I forget how much, were stolen. At the case in court the fellow in question got off, on the plea that anyone might have entered from the street, since the College gate was open and Wystan's door unlocked. The easy acquittal may be regarded as much characteristic of our slack society as the breach of trust itself. A number of noted Christians among dons were taken advantage of in this way by a group eventually brought to book.

Of course some people misinterpreted the affair, and blamed Wystan: they were quite wrong, as I can aver. He was quite blameless in the matter, except in being too Christian and too confiding in humans. (Historians know better what they are.) But it was a bad start, that he should have come away from New York to be burgled in Oxford, and it was an ill omen for his return.

That year he produced a volume, *Epistle to a Godson and Other Poems*, which he gave me, inscribed 'With love from Wystan' – I thought, how nice of him after all the years! The epigraph gives us a clue to it:

> at Twenty I tried to
> vex my elders, past Sixty it's the young whom
> I hope to bother.

(Fancy his caring! I don't even hope that much – in such a society, it's not worth it.)

The title poem – for Stephen Spender's young son – expresses the poet's nostalgia for the better society of the past and his fears for the future:

> who am I to avouch for any Christian
> baby, far less offer ghostly platitudes
> to a young man? In yester times it
> was different: the old could still be helpful

> when they could nicely envisage the future
> as a named and settled landscape their children
> would make the same sense of as they did,
> laughing and weeping at the same stories.

Now – 'You don't need me to tell you what's/going on ... the ochlocratic [mob-ruled] media/process and vent without inter-mission/all today's ugly secrets ... if what is to happen/occurs according to what Thucydides/defined as "human", we've had it, are in for/a disaster that no four-letter/words will tardy. ...' He was thinking of the possibility of nuclear disaster, the shadow that lies upon us all in this appalling century. It might be Swift writing – but Swift did not have to contemplate, even in imagination, destruction of life on a planetary scale.

Nor did Auden let up in his condemnation in subsequent poems:

> We all ask, but I doubt if anyone
> can really say why all age-groups should find our
> Age quite so repulsive ...

There are some in my age-group who can say why. Then

> Housman was perfectly right.
> Our world rapidly worsens:
> nothing is now so horrid
> or silly it can't occur.

Housman had no illusions, any more than Hardy had – safer, in such a time, to entertain no illusions. Oddly enough, even in my Leftist days, I had few illusions: Liberal illusions are a middle-class phenomenon: they are not characteristic of the working class – Auden had to outgrow them. (Isherwood took refuge in high-minded humbug.) I think we may regard the poem, a series of shorts, 'I Am Not a Camera', as scoring Isherwood's *I Am a Camera*, for which he received such acclaim as a photographic realist. Wystan quotes an epigraph in contradiction: 'The photographable life is always either trivial or already sterilised.' One of the shorts, in Japanese haiku form, clinches the matter:

> The camera may
> do justice to laughter, but must
> degrade sorrow.

In these later poems Auden comes out from his earlier reserve, and gives the personal a proper ride. 'Talking to Myself' is completely, necessarily autobiographical. He confesses to being, what we have guessed all along, 'instinctively passive'. Addressing himself as You:

> I looked at Your looks askance. *His architecture*
> *should have been much more imposing: I've been let down!*

In spite of these disadvantages,

> For many years
> You were, I admit, a martyr to horn-colic
> (it did no good to tell You. *But I'm not in love!*)

We may diagnose here: over-sexed in desire, while under-equipped for it, always a predisposing itch to compensate in achievement – as it was with Napoleon.

He was lucky, considering how much he had exposed himself, to be able to say:

how stoutly, though, You've repelled all germ invasions,

(Isherwood, for all his assumed sanctity, hadn't.)

but never chastised my tantrums with a megrim.

(Nor me – amid all my duodenal anguish, never a headache.) When he looked round at the horrors of today,

when I read the papers, You seem an Adonis.

There was Wystan's secret wish, to have been an Adonis. Here was the hidden, gnawing sense of disappointment, providing another itch to achieve. His last wish was however granted: when it came to the end,

pay no attention
to my piteous *Don'ts*, but bugger off quickly.

And Spender was able, with this elegant phrase, to conclude his valediction in Christ Church cathedral.

We need hardly go further to note Auden's reversal from his youthful self: common sense had always been there, and at length broke through.

Wild horses could not drag me to debates on
Art and Society:

(which Stephen wasted so much time on, *pour faute de mieux*)

critics with credos,
Christian or Marxist, should keep their trap shut,
Lest they spout nonsense.

> Dare any call Permissiveness
> An educational success?
> Saner those class-rooms which I sat in,
> Compelled to study Greek and Latin.

He had never been so ungrateful to the poor prep-school teachers who had done their best for them as Orwell and Connolly were (Connolly had the later decency to apologise to them).

> I cannot settle which is worse,
> The Anti-Novel or Free Verse.

A master of every conceivable verse-form, even when the result is not poetry, he would have no respect for the uncooked and formless idiom of most contemporary outpourings – any more than Betjeman or Larkin had (and Eliot didn't care for much post-Eliot poetry).

Auden ended up, as against abstractions and woolly theorising,

> I feel
> Most at home with what is Real.

And I feel a particular agreement with his sentiment:

> A poet's hope: to be,
> like some valley cheese,
> local, but prized elsewhere.

Auden's last volume, *Thank You, Fog*, continues these themes; one observes life closing in around him. The title poem thanks a whole week of fog in Wiltshire at Christmas for insulating him and his friends there from the horrors of the world outside:

> No summer sun will ever
> dismantle the global gloom
> cast by the Daily Papers

– how much I agree –

> vomiting in slipshod prose
> the facts of filth and violence
> that we're too dumb to prevent.

In 'A Curse',

> Dark was that when Diesel
> conceived his grim engine that
> begot you, vile invention,
> more vicious, more criminal
> than the camera even . . .

The book contains a short anti-masque, a last dramatic piece written with Kallman, 'The Entertainment of the Senses', commissioned by the hospitable (for him) Arts Council of Great Britain, set to music and performed at the Queen Elizabeth Hall. One recognises the old boys – Chester, though fourteen years younger, was ageing as much as Wystan, from a spendthrift life – in an earlier theme:

> When you see a fair form, chase it
> And if possible embrace it,
> Be it a girl or a boy.
> Don't be bashful: be brash, be fresh.
> Life is short, so enjoy
> Whatever contact your flesh
> May at the moment crave:
> There's no sex-life in the grave.

Then this not very cheerful piece turns to satire on the time: the young lovers are bidden

> To talk, talk, talk, talk
> With your Transistors on as you walk

– as one hears them everywhere in public places, filling the vacuum of their minds – as it might be in Christ Church Meadows or on the river.

> For the prissy minority
> Who prefer a low sonority
> There's only one thing to be done:
> Become a Trappist or a nun.
> Let them. Come, girls and boys,
> More noise, more noise!
> Yell while you can and save
> Your silence for the grave.

At the end of the piece:

> The moral is, as they have said,
> Be With-it, With-it, With-it, till you're dead.

It would seem that he ended up with no more liking for such a society than I have.

A more agreeable – and informative – subject is provided by an autobiographical poem, 'A Thanksgiving', which gives us the story of his own artistic development. We might append to that the moral that, in so grievous a time, more satisfaction is to be had by looking within than without: my own gospel of solipsism.

> Thus, when I started to verse,
> I presently sat at the feet of
> *Hardy* and *Thomas* and *Frost*.

There could not be better guides for a beginner.

> Falling in love altered that,
> now Someone, at least, was important:
> *Yeats* was a help, so was *Graves*.

Later, he disclaimed Yeats: he came to feel that his influence had encouraged the false rhetoric in the early poems. He went through them rigorously reducing that element where he could, his aim having become 'the sober truthfulness of prose with a poetic unique-ness of expression', and with that, 'a deliberate avoidance of visual imagery.' I regard this last as a mistaken idea: he was already sufficiently weak visually. He could have done with more, not less.

In Berlin, in the world economic depression he picked up the influence of Brecht, whom he eventually came to regard as the horrible man he was. The influence is strongest upon *The Dog Beneath the Skin*, with its mixture of *genres*. Next, the horrors unleashed by Hitler and Stalin

> forced me to think about God.
>
> Why was I sure they were wrong?
> Wild *Kierkegaard*, *Williams* and *Lewis*
> guided me back to belief.

A little common sense was all that was necessary to tell one that Hitler and Stalin were not merely wrong but evil. As for belief, I do not think that Auden was intellectually strong enough to formulate a position of his own, any more than Betjeman was; and Larkin, without it, was miserable. Carpenter tells us that early and late Auden disclaimed the 'Wordsworthian nostalgia' for the world of nature. This was short-sighted of him in both senses; for at the very least the beauty of the external world is a constant consolation and a remedy for despair. It can perhaps be even more, and put one in touch with something beyond the temporal and the world of sense.

I dare be so unfashionable as to prefer a youthful poem of Auden's, before he became mature and sophisticated – sophistication can be an enemy. Here is a stanza from an early Elegy, on a schoolboy killed by a fall from a tree:

> No dog barked in the street below
> The churchyard where they dug his grave,
> The day wore nothing strange to show
> The earth took back the dust she gave,
> And cuckoos they were calling still
> When we had left him in the hill.

Remember Hardy: poetry is what moves the *heart*, expressed in such a way as to move other hearts.

The return to Oxford was not the success it had been a dozen or more years before. Auden had grown older and odder; a new generation had come up that did not much want to hear what he had to say – after all, he had said it all before. That should not have saddened him – he could have consoled himself, as I do, with Henry James's 'Nobody ever understands *any*thing', and simply not have cared what anybody thinks; it is usually nonsense, on whatever subject. But he was not the man to retire into the shell of scholarship and solitude, like Housman – my model.

He missed too the traditional ritual of Common Room life, with the multiplication of numbers. (It survived better, if rather over-burdened, at All Souls.) Dons were busier men, with no time to linger over port, or even to come into Common Room after dinner for dessert – and family life (ugh!) called. Wystan was left lonelier than he had expected.

I should have gone over to the brewhouse to see him, but it really didn't occur to me – I found working away on my own sufficient. Wystan, like a public school man, was gregarious and sociable, not good at getting along without company. (As an undergraduate at Christ Church, I could not understand the public school boys always in each other's rooms: how could they get any work done? I was only too happy to have at last a room of my own.) Wystan longed to have something like a family around him. He was reduced to singing a 'Lullaby' to himself:

> The din of work is subdued:
> another day has westered,
> and mantling darkness arrived.
> Now you have licence to lie
> naked, curled like a shrimplet . . .
> snug in the den of yourself . . .
> Sleep, Big Baby, sleep your fill.

All the same, it was rather a surprise, when he said to me one day at All Souls, that seventy was the right age to die, and I suddenly saw that he did not want to go on living.

He could not live without love: it is an obsession all through his life and work. Even at the end he was writing,

> Man must either fall in love
> with Someone or something
> or else fall ill.

Love is central to life, but it is not all or everything, and it is very far from occupying the whole area of anyone's life. Many people can do without it or have to do without it, others do not even want it or have other interests in lieu of it. Wystan did not allow for the enormous area not occupied by love, or even sex – a lot of people are undersexed or just not interested. Though intimately connected, they are not the same thing, though often enough Wystan confused the two in his writing. Nevertheless, he was capable of both Eros and Agape, pagan Amor and Christian Caritas – overwhelmingly evident in his protective, self-sacrificing, forbearing relationship with Chester. No wonder I always regarded Wystan as a good man, a Christian gentleman.

When he died, Chester said, 'I've lost my criterion', and survived him by only six months.

All the same, what an extraordinary story it is, and how very modern – like a modern morality. It stands out all the more strange when one thinks of it in the perspective of the lives of other poets – Shakespeare or Milton, Wordsworth or Coleridge, Arnold, Browning, Hardy, Yeats, Kipling – almost any of them. True, Byron was bisexual, and Tennyson deeply in love with Arthur Hallam, though entirely platonically. Modern poets are almost another species: would their precursors recognise them, even as poets?

Was Auden a 'great' poet?

In the course of writing this book my mind has gone up and down about that, though I have a consistent reading of him in other ways. To achieve greatness in poetry it must be (a) universal and (b) permanent, at least lasting. As to the second, we cannot tell. Auden's range was phenomenally wide, his genius achieved complete expression in his work, but was it universal?

Is it significant that Eliot refers to Auden's work as 'verse', the term he used for Kipling's? Indeed, there is something in common between Auden and Kipling, both brash, both rhetoricians. Neither of them wrote much in Valéry's sense of 'la poésie pure'. Edwin Muir – a fine poet himself (more congenial to me) and a just critic – thought that Auden may have been too much the poet of his particular age. All I can say is that I am glad to have lived along with him in the age, if only marginally in his company, at least a constant companion in his work.

About the Author

A.L. Rowse is both poet and man of letters as well as historian, and has the Benson medal of the Royal Society of Literature for his literary work. He was the Douglas Jerrold Scholar in English Literature at Christ Church, Oxford, just before Auden came up there as exhibitioner in Natural Science. Paradoxically, Auden took to literature while Rowse concentrated more on history—thus becoming a Fellow of All Souls, and of the British Academy—while maintaining his primary interest in literature and writing poetry.